THE COMPLETE
COCKTAIL
MAKER

THE COMPLETE
COCKTAIL MAKER

A professional bartender's guide to over 500 classic
and contemporary mixed drinks – showing how to
create them, with helpful step-by-step instructions

STUART WALTON

southwater

This edition is published by Southwater

Southwater is an imprint of Anness Publishing Ltd
Hermes House, 88–89 Blackfriars Road, London SE1 8HA
tel. 020 7401 2077; fax 020 7633 9499
www.southwaterbooks.com; www.annesspublishing.com

If you like the images in this book and would like to investigate using them for publishing, promotions or advertising, please visit our website www.practicalpictures.com for more information.

UK agent: The Manning Partnership Ltd, 6 The Old Dairy, Melcombe Road, Bath BA2 3LR; tel. 01225 478444; fax 01225 478440; sales@manning-partnership.co.uk

UK distributor: Grantham Book Services Ltd, Isaac Newton Way, Alma Park Industrial Estate, Grantham, Lincs NG31 9SD; tel. 01476 541080; fax 01476 541061; orders@gbs.tbs-ltd.co.uk

North American agent/distributor: National Book Network, 4501 Forbes Boulevard, Suite 200, Lanham, MD 20706; tel. 301 459 3366; fax 301 429 5746; www.nbnbooks.com

Australian agent/distributor: Pan Macmillan Australia, Level 18, St Martins Tower, 31 Market St, Sydney, NSW 2000; tel. 1300 135 113; fax 1300 135 103; customer.service@macmillan.com.au

New Zealand agent/distributor: David Bateman Ltd, 30 Tarndale Grove, Off Bush Road, Albany, Auckland; tel. (09) 415 7664; fax (09) 415 8892

A CIP catalogue record for this book is available from the British Library.

Publisher: Joanna Lorenz
Editorial Director: Judith Simons
Project Editor: Felicity Forster
Photographers: Frank Adam, Steve Baxter and Janine Hosegood
Designer: Nigel Partridge
Copy Editor: Kate Humby
Editorial Reader: Jay Thundercliffe
Production Controller: Don Campaniello

Previously published as part of a larger volume, *The Complete Guide to Cocktails and Drinks*

CONTENTS

INTRODUCTION

At what point in history someone first used an alcoholic substance to fulfil what would become its time-honoured role as intoxicant is a question that may never be answered. What is certain is that the first such use arose from the discovery of the effects of fermentation on either fruit, honey or sticky-sweet palm sap.

First alcohol

The ancient Egyptians used fermented grains for making prototype forms of beer. These grains also enabled them to refine the techniques for producing raised breads. They found that adding beer sediment – which was still full of live yeasts – was the quickest and easiest method of encouraging the start of fermentation in a new batch of dough.

Below: This Egyptian figure dates from c.2450–2290 BC, and shows a woman at a mixing tub making beer.

Wine came after beer, but was to become of crucial cultural and religious importance to the civilizations of Egypt, and classical Greece and Rome. It was used as a sacrament in orgiastic celebrations of the festivals of Dionysos, the Greek god of nature (Bacchus to the Romans). From such ancient rituals, the first public performances recognizable as drama are said to have evolved.

In addition to its ceremonial and cultural role, wine was also used for culinary purposes. Not only was it capable of making tough meat more supple, but wine marinades would have removed excess salt from meats that had been encrusted with salt, or soaked in brine, for preservation. Wine vinegar, its alcohol lost to acetic acid, may have been the first recourse, but wine itself appears in sauce recipes in the historically important late Roman cookbook of Apicius (3rd century AD). The wine itself was commonly infused with spices to mask the rank flavours of oxidation or acetification.

Distillation

The next important step was the discovery of the art of distilling. Distillation (from the Latin *destillare*; to drip) is the extraction of higher alcohols from fermented drinks, which uses the action of heat to vaporize them. Compared to fermentation, distillation is a remarkably simple process, largely because it is much easier to control. Whereas freshly pressed grape juice needs the right ambient temperature to begin the process of turning into wine, a spirit can be produced from wine simply by applying heat to it.

Alcohol has a lower boiling point than water (about 78°C/172°F, compared to 100°C/212°F), so it vaporizes into steam some time before the water content in the wine starts to boil. When the alcohol-laden steam hits a cool surface, it forms a dripping condensation, and reverts to a liquid with a much higher proportion of alcohol than the wine. Boil that liquid

up again, and the same procedure will yield an even higher alcohol, and so on.

Much academic debate has been generated in the last 30 years or so as to when and where distillation was first discovered. The Greek philosopher Aristotle, who lived in the 4th century BC, writes of distillation as a way of purifying seawater to make it drinkable. He comments in passing that the same treatment can be given to wine, which is reduced thereby to a sort of "water". He was tantalizingly close to a breakthrough, but his experiment did no more than prove that wine is just a form of modified water, and that a liquid can only derive flavour from whatever happens to be mixed with the water that forms its base.

The documented beginnings of systematic and scientifically founded distillation, at least in Europe, come from the celebrated medical school at Salerno around AD 1100. Wine itself was held to have a range of medicinal properties (a view that found favour again in the 1990s), and the extraction of what was held to be the soul or spirit of the wine, through distillation, is what led to the naming of distillates as "spirits".

Alcohol and alchemy

Alcohol was believed to be the active ingredient in the healing powers of wine. Up to that time, the word "alcohol" was applied as a generic term to any product derived through vaporization and condensation. Its origin from the Arabic word *al-kuhl* refers to the Arab practice of producing a black powder by condensing a vapour of the metal antimony. The powder was then used as eye make-up, which is why eye-liner is still occasionally known as kohl. It was not until some time during the 16th century that "alcohol" was used specifically in reference to distilled spirits.

Not only medicine but the ancient practice of alchemy were involved in the European origins of distillation. Alchemy was a respected branch of the physical

Above: A vase painting from c.460–450 BC, showing Greeks sharing a drink at a banquet. Note the flat drinking vessel.

sciences, and was chiefly concerned with finding a means of transforming ordinary metals into gold. People wholeheartedly believed that if such a process could be discovered, it might well be possible to apply it to the human body and extract the essential life force from its mortal shell, thus guaranteeing eternal youth. With the realization that alcohol could be repeatedly distilled to ever-greater levels of purity, people came to believe that spirits could be the Holy Grail.

It can't have taken long for the Salerno doctors to ascertain that, whatever other remarkable properties distilled spirit had, the power to confer everlasting life wasn't one of them. However, the medical applications of spirits were to endure for hundreds of years. It was Arnaldo de Vilanova, a Catalan physician of the 13th century,

Right: This 15th-century English illustration shows scientists preparing for an alchemical experiment.

who first coined the Latin term *aqua vitae*, "water of life", for distilled spirits, indicating that they were associated with the promotion of vitality and health. (That term lives on in the Scandinavian *aquavit* and the French *eau de vie*, as well as the names of various other spirits.)

First distillates

Undoubtedly, the earliest distillates were of wine, since it had a more salubrious and exalted image than beer; grain

distillation to produce the first whiskies and neutral spirits followed in the Middle Ages. Many of these prototypes contained herb and spice extracts, or were flavoured with fruit, in order to enhance the medicinal properties of the preparation. The additives also conveniently masked what must have been the fairly raw taste and off-putting aroma of the unadulterated liquor.

Anyone who has smelt and tasted clear spirit dripping off the still in a brandy distillery (or, for that matter, has had a brush with illicit Irish poteen or American moonshine) will know how far removed untreated spirit is from the welcoming smoothness of five-star cognac or single malt Scotch. The infused distillates were the antecedents of many of the traditional aromatic liqueurs and flavoured vodkas of today.

Such, for centuries, was the official account of the birth of distilled spirits. In 1961, however, an Indian food historian, O. Prakash, argued that there was evidence that distillation of rice and barley beer was practised in India as early as 800 BC. Others have argued that, if this was so, then distillation probably arrived there from China even

Above: This late 14th-century Italian manuscript shows people enjoying their wine in an upper room, with the cellarman hard at work in the wine cellar below.

earlier. Thus, current theory cautiously credits the Chinese as the discoverers of the art.

It seems unusual that distilled alcohol was not remarked on or, apparently even encountered by soldiers engaged in the European invasion of India, led by Alexander the Great in 327 BC. His campaign is reliably credited with having brought rice back to Europe, but any rice spirit appears to have been overlooked. Perhaps, if it was drunk at all by the invaders, it was in a diluted form, and was therefore not perceived to be any higher in alcohol than the grape wine with which they were familiar. Then again, it may just have been rejected as smelling or looking unclean. Whatever the explanation, if the Chinese or Indians did practise distillation as long ago as is claimed, the expertise they had stumbled on centuries before the Europeans remained specific to that part of the world. Thus did the course of history remain tantalizingly unchanged.

Distillation methods

The original and widespread distillation vessel, still used in the Cognac region of France and by the whisky distillers of Scotland, is the pot still. It consists of the only three elements absolutely essential to the process: a pot in which the fermented product (malted grains, wine, cider, etc.) is heated; the alembic, or tube, through which the alcohol vapour driven off is sucked up; and the condenser, where the steam is cooled and reliquefied. To obtain a better quality product, spirits are generally distilled at least twice for greater refinement, so the still has to be started up again.

Not all the condensed vapour is suitable for use in fine liquor. The first and last of it to pass through (known as the "heads" and "tails") are generally discarded, because of the relatively high level of impurities they contain. The invention of the continuous still in the early 19th century, in which the process carries on to a second distillation uninterrupted, made spirit production more economical and easier to control. This is the method used in France's other classic brandy, armagnac, and the continuous still is now the preferred apparatus for the production of most spirits worldwide.

Below: Distillation in Strasburg, Germany, during the 16th century.

Spirits

Probably the first spirit to be taken seriously as an object of connoisseurship, as distinct from being purely medicinal or just a method of using up surplus grape or grain production, was the brandy of the Cognac region of western France. People noticed that the superior, mellower spirit produced by the light wines of Cognac responded particularly well to ageing in oak casks. The casks were traditionally fashioned out of wood from the Limousin forests of the region.

Cask-aged spirits derive every aspect of their final character – from the precise shade of tawny in the colour to their richness and roundness of flavour – from the maturation period they undergo in wood. They will not continue to develop in the bottle. The complex classification system in operation today for cognac is based on the length of time the spirit has been aged. It is testimony to a reputation for painstaking quality that dates back to around the end of the 17th century.

Scottish and Irish whiskies rose to similar prominence soon after this date. Their differing production processes resulted in quite distinct regional styles, depending on the quantities of peat used in the kilns where the malted grain is dried, on the quality of the spring water used in the mash and, some have claimed, on the shape of the still. Varieties of whisky are made across the world these days, from North America to Japan, but all attempts to replicate the precise taste of great Scotch – despite the use of identical ingredients and procedures – have somehow inexplicably foundered.

Liqueurs

Where a distilled drink stops being a spirit and turns into a liqueur is something of an elusive question. The one constant is that, to be a liqueur, a drink should have some obvious aromatizing element (perhaps even a hundred or more in the case of certain celebrated products). This doesn't mean that all flavoured distillates are liqueurs – flavoured vodkas are still vodka – but there are no neutral liqueurs. Some of these products have histories at least as venerable as those of cognac and Scotch. The most notable are those produced by the old French monastic orders. Bénédictine, the cognac-based, herb-scented potion that originated at the monastery in Fécamp, in Normandy, can convincingly lay claim to a lineage that rolls back to the beginning of the 16th century.

The first and greatest cocktail era, which arrived with the advent of the Jazz Age in the 1920s, rescued many of the traditional liqueurs from the niches of obscurity into which they had been relegated by popular taste. The Benedictine monks may have been a little shocked to hear that their revered creation was being mixed with English gin, American applejack, apricot brandy and maple syrup, and then shaken to within an inch of its life and renamed

Below: Cognac ageing in barrels at Courvoisier in Jarnac.

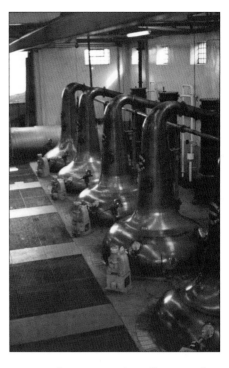

Right: Modern whisky stills at the Glenfiddich distillery in Scotland.

the Mule's Hind Leg, but at least it was drunk – as were the giggling flappers after recklessly knocking back three or four of them.

How to use this book

In the first section of this book, we look at what equipment is needed – from shakers and measures to the many different types of glasses and their uses – and what tricks and techniques should be learned for successful home bartending. We also take a good look at garnishes, so that your drinks will look the part as well as taste it. Whether you are throwing a cocktail party, or whether you just want to know how to make cocktails as good as – if not much better than – those you have tasted in the cocktail bar, all the information you need is here.

Then, getting down to business, the second part of the book consists of over 500 cocktail recipes, arranged by type, so that you can happily expand your repertoire. That drink after work or on a Saturday night need no longer be the same old bottle of beer, glass of wine or G&T. The drinking world is your oyster. Do it wisely, and have fun.

Bartending techniques

In this part of the book, we shall find out what props and paraphernalia are needed to set up your own professional-looking bartending operation at home. After going through the bartender's equipment, and types of glasses and garnishes commonly used, we'll learn how to measure, mix and pour, and how to plan and carry off a successful cocktail party. We'll end with some useful advice on avoiding or mitigating the unwanted after-effects of such an occasion.

Bartending equipment

To make a successful cocktail bartender, you will need a few essential pieces of equipment. The most vital and flamboyant is the cocktail shaker, but what you have on hand in the kitchen can usually stand in for the rest. After a while, though, you may find the urge to invest in some of the following specialist pieces of equipment.

Measuring jug
Cocktail shakers usually come with standard measures for apportioning out the ingredients. These may be small cups, or something shaped like a double trumpet, one side of which is a whole measure, the other half. If you don't have one, then use a jug for measuring out the required quantities. The measurements can be in single (25ml/1fl oz) or double (50ml/2fl oz) bar measures. Do not switch from one type of measurement to another within the same recipe.

Below: Measuring jug and spoon measures.

Left: Cocktail shaker.

Below: Measure.

Measure
Be sure to buy a shaker that comes with a measure, known in American parlance as a "jigger". They usually come as a single-piece double cup, with one side a whole measure and the other a half. Once you have established the capacity of the two sides, you will save a great deal of bother apportioning out ingredients in a measuring jug. It also looks a lot more professional than using spoons.

Cocktail shaker
The shaker is used for drinks that need good mixing, but don't have to be crystal-clear. Once the ingredients have been thoroughly amalgamated in the presence of ice, the temperature clouds up the drink. Cocktail shakers are usually made of stainless steel, but can also be silver, hard plastic or tough glass. The Boston shaker is made of two cup-type containers that fit over each other, one normally made of glass, the other

of metal. This type is often preferred by professional bartenders. For beginners, the classic three-piece shaker is easier to handle, with its base to hold the ice and liquids, a top fitted with a built-in strainer and a tight-fitting cap. Make sure you hold on to that cap while you are shaking. As a rough rule, the drink is ready when the shaker has become almost too painfully cold to hold, which is generally not more than around 15–20 seconds.

Blender or liquidizer
Goblet blenders are the best shape for mixing cocktails that need to be aerated, as well as for creating frothy cocktails or ones made with finely crushed ice. Attempting to break up whole ice cubes in the blender may very well blunt the blades. Opt for an

Below: Blender.

ice bag or tea-towel, a rolling pin and plenty of brute force, or better still, use an ice crusher.

Ice bags

These plastic bags that can be filled with water and frozen are a kind of disposable ice tray. You simply press each piece of ice out of them, tearing through the plastic as you go. They also have the advantage of making a more rounded piece of ice, as opposed to the hard-angled cube that an ice tray produces.

Ice crusher

If the prospect of breaking up ice with a hammer and dish towel comes to seem almost as much of a penance as working on a chain gang, an ice-crushing machine is the answer. It comes in two parts. You fill the top with whole ice cubes, put the lid on and, while pressing down on the top, turn the gramophone-type handle on the

Below: Wooden hammer and towel.

side. Take the top half off to retrieve the crystals of ice "snow" from the lower part. Crushed ice is used to fill the glasses for drinks that are to be served frappé. It naturally melts very quickly, though, compared to cubes.

Wooden hammer

Use a wooden hammer for crushing ice. The end of a wooden rolling pin works just as well.

Ice bag or towel

A towel or bag is essential for holding ice cubes when crushing, whether you are creating roughly cracked lumps or a fine snow. It must be scrupulously clean and fresh for each repeated use.

Ice bucket and chiller bucket

An ice bucket with a close-fitting lid is useful if you are going to be making several cocktails in quick succession. They are not completely hermetic though, and ice will eventually melt in them, albeit a little more slowly

than if left at room temperature. It should not be confused with a chiller bucket for bottles of champagne and white wine, which is bigger and has handles on the sides, but doesn't have a lid. A chiller bucket is intended to be filled with iced water, as opposed to ice alone.

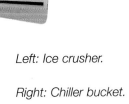

Left: Ice crusher.

Right: Chiller bucket.

Above: Mixing pitcher and muddlers.

Above: Bar spoon.

Hawthorn strainer, is made from stainless steel and looks like a flat spoon with holes and a curl of wire on the underside. It is held over the top of the glass to keep the ice and any other solid ingredients back.

Corkscrew

The fold-up type of corkscrew is known as the Waiter's Friend, and incorporates a can opener and bottle-top flipper as well as the screw itself. It is the most useful version to have to hand as it suits all purposes. The spin-handled corkscrew with a blade for cutting foil is the best one for opening fine wines.

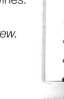

Right: Corkscrew.

Mixing pitcher or bar glass

It is useful to have a container in which to mix and stir drinks that are not shaken. The glass or pitcher should be large enough to hold two or three drinks. This vessel is intended for drinks that are meant to be clear, not cloudy.

Muddler

A long stick with a bulbous end, the muddler is used for crushing sugar or mint leaves, and so is particularly useful when creating juleps or smashes. A variety of sizes is available. It should be used like a pestle in a mixing jug; the smaller version is for use in an individual glass. At a pinch, a flattish spoon can be used instead of a muddler, but then you will find it more awkward to

Right: Strainer.

apply sideways rather than downward pressure when trying to press those mint leaves.

Bar spoon

These long-handled spoons can reach to the bottom of the tallest tumblers and are used in jugs, or for mixing the drink directly in the glass. Some varieties look like a large swizzle-stick, with a long handle and a disc at one end. They also look considerably more elegant than a dessert spoon.

Strainer

Used for pouring drinks from a shaker or mixing jug into a cocktail glass, the strainer's function is to remove the ice with which the drink has been prepared. Some drinks are served with the ice in (or "on the rocks") but most aren't, the reason being that you don't want the ice to unhelpfully dilute the drink. The best strainer, known professionally as a

Sharp knife and squeezer

Citrus fruit is essential in countless cocktails. A good quality, sharp knife is required for halving the fruit, and the squeezer for extracting its juice. Although fruit juice presses are quicker to use, they are more expensive and more boring to wash up afterwards.

Below: Sharp knife and squeezer.

Left: Nutmeg grater.

Right: Zester and canelle knife.

USING A ZESTER

Hold the citrus fruit firmly in one hand, and peel away short or long strips of the skin as desired with the other. The pared-away skin makes a delicate garnish that floats on the surface of a drink.

Nutmeg grater

A tiny grater with small holes, for grating nutmeg over egg-nogs, frothy and creamy drinks. If this sounds too fiddly, buy ready-ground nutmeg instead. It's almost as good.

Zester and canelle knife

These are used for presenting fruit attractively to garnish glasses. If you don't already have them, don't feel obliged to run out and buy them, since drinks can look equally attractive with simply sliced fruit. The zester has a row of tiny holes that remove the top layer of skin off a citrus fruit when dragged across it (although the finest gauge on your multi-purpose grater was also designed for just this job). A canelle knife (from the French word for a "channel" or "groove") is for making decorative stripes in the skins of a whole fruit. When sliced, they then have a groovy-looking serrated edge. It is, in effect, a narrow-gauged version of a traditional potato peeler, but is purely for decorative purposes.

Egg whisk

Use a whisk to beat a little frothy texture into egg white before you add it to the shaker. It helps the texture of the finished drink no end. An ordinary balloon whisk will do the trick, although for culinary uses, a rotary whisk with a handle (or the electric specimen) is best.

Straws, swizzle-sticks and cocktail sticks

These decorative items are used to add the finishing touches to a cocktail. It was once considered axiomatic to drink all cocktails through straws. They tend now to be the exception rather than the rule. The flavours of the drink are better appreciated if it is poured directly into the mouth, as opposed to being sucked up in a thin stream. A mythical belief that the alcohol took effect more quickly if taken through straws was responsible for their popularity in the 1980s.

A swizzle-stick is useful for stirring a drink, and may be substituted by such food items as a stick of celery in a Bloody Mary, or a length of whole cinnamon for a short creamy cocktail or a hot, spicy drink such as mulled wine or ale.

Cocktail sticks are purely decorative and are used for holding ingredients such as cherries or other items of fruit that would otherwise sink to the bottom of the glass.

And if you intend to eat the cherry or olive, it's handier if it's already speared, so that you don't have to commit the appalling faux pas of dipping a finger into the drink to catch it.

Left: Swizzle-sticks.

Above: Egg whisk.

Right: Cocktail sticks.

Glasses

To ensure that glasses are sparkling clean, they should always be washed and dried with a glass cloth. Although some recipes suggest chilled glasses, don't put best crystal in the freezer; leave it at the back of the refrigerator instead. An hour should be enough.

Cocktail glass or Martini glass

This elegant glass is a wide conical bowl on a tall stem: a design that keeps cocktails cool by keeping warm hands away from the drink. It is by far the most widely used glass, so a set is essential. The design belies the fact that the capacity of this glass is relatively small (about three standard measures). Uses: the classic Martini and its variations, and almost any short, sharp, strong cocktail, including creamy ones.

Collins glass

The tallest of the tumblers, narrow with perfectly straight sides, a Collins glass holds about 350ml/12fl oz, and is usually used for serving long drinks made with fresh juices or finished with a sparkling mixer such as soda. This glass can also stand in as the highball glass, which is traditionally slightly less tall. Uses: Tom Collins, and all drinks that are to be "topped up" with anything.

Old-fashioned glass, tumbler or rocks glass

Classic, short whisky tumblers are used for shorter drinks, served on the rocks, and generally for drinks that are stirred rather than shaken. They should hold about 250ml/8fl oz. Uses: Old-Fashioned, Manhattan, Sours, etc.

Liqueur glass

Tiny liqueur glasses were traditionally used to serve small measures of unmixed drinks, and hold no more than 80ml/3fl oz. They are a good alternative for making a pousse-café or layered cocktail. They are best not used for serving measures of fortified wines such as sherry, port and madeira, where they will look ridiculously mean.

Above: Tumbler.   *Above: Liqueur glass.*

Brandy balloon or snifter

The brandy glass is designed to trap the fragrance of the brandy in the bowl of the glass. Cupping the glass in the palm of the hand further helps to warm it gently and release its aromas. Not now considered the thing to use for best cognac, it nonetheless makes a good cocktail glass for certain short, strong drinks that have been stirred rather than shaken. The wide bowl makes them suitable for drinks with solids floating in them.

Below: Large cocktail glass.

Below: Collins glass.

Below: Cocktail glass.

Below: Brandy balloon.

Above: Champagne flute.   *Above: Champagne saucer.*   *Above: Red wine glass.*   *Above: White wine glass.*

Large cocktail goblet or poco

Available in various sizes and shapes, large cocktail goblets are good for serving larger frothy drinks, or drinks containing puréed fruit or coconut cream. Classically, they are the glasses for Piña Coladas. The wider rims leave plenty of room for flamboyant and colourful decorations.

Champagne flute

The champagne flute is the more acceptable glass to use for quality sparkling wines. It is more efficient at conserving the bubbles since there is less surface area for them to break on. It should be used for champagne cocktails too. Always choose one with good depth, as the shorter ones look too parsimonious.

Champagne saucer

The old-fashioned saucer glass may be frowned on now for champagne, but it is an attractive and elegant design and can be used for a number of cocktails, particularly those that have cracked ice floating in them. Because of the wider surface area, there is plenty of scope for fruity garnishes too.

Red wine glass

The most useful size of wine glass, the red wine glass holds about 500ml/ 16fl oz. It should only be filled about a third full to allow the wine to be swirled around, so that it releases its bouquet. It can be used for long wine cocktails too, and will do at a pinch as a stand-in for the large cocktail goblet.

White wine glass

A long-stemmed, medium-sized glass of about 250ml/8fl oz capacity, a white wine glass should be held by the stem so as not to warm the chilled wine or cocktail with the heat of the hand. Use it for short wine cocktails such as spritzers and wine-based punches.

Pousse-café

A thin and narrow glass standing on a short stem, a pousse-café is used for floating or layering liqueurs one on top of the other. If you haven't got one, use a liqueur glass or even an old-fashioned sherry schooner instead. This is not a type of drink you are likely to be making very often. Although they look impressive, the novelty does rather wear off.

Shot glass

A tiny glass with a capacity of no more than 50ml/2fl oz, the shot glass is used for those very short, lethally strong cocktails known as shooters. If you're going to make a shooter, this is absolutely the only glass to use. No substitute will be accepted. The glass itself is usually extremely thick, as these drinks are intended to be thrown back in one, and then the glass slammed down fairly peremptorily on the bar counter. Go for it.

Below: Pousse-café.

Below: Shot glass.

Garnishes

It is far more elegant not to overdress cocktails, otherwise they all too quickly turn into a fruit salad with a drink attached. Less is best. The edible extras suggested on these pages add colour, flavour and visual interest to any glass.

Frosting

Frosting glasses with salt, sugar or cocoa is a simple but effective touch. It is extremely quick and easy, and means that the drink needs no other decoration.

Salt is absolutely indispensable for frosting the rim of a textbook Margarita, and is normally done with lime juice. For a sweet drink, sugar frosting makes for an appealingly festive look. It is appropriate for drinks such as Royal Silver, Golden Start and Brandy Crusta.

Left: Many kinds of sugar can be added to drinks: soft brown, demerara, dark muscovado, sugar cubes, cane sugar and caster (superfine) sugar.

SALT

A traditional Margarita should always have salt around the rim of the glass. To do this, rub the rim of the glass with a wedge of fresh lime and then dip the glass in fine salt. This example has an additional twist of cucumber rind as a garnish – but try not to over-garnish your drinks. Less is more.

SUGAR AND SYRUP

This champagne saucer was dipped into a shallow bowl of grenadine, then dipped into caster (superfine) sugar to create a frosted rim. The grenadine makes the sugar go bright pink. The glass was then placed in the refrigerator so that it was well chilled before being filled.

SUGAR AND FRUIT JUICE

It is possible to frost a glass with any fruit that goes with the drink. For example, this drink consists of Galliano mixed with a variety of fruit juices and coconut cream. The rim of the glass has been dipped in pineapple juice, then covered in a fine coating of caster (superfine) sugar.

Alternatively, a dark brown frosting of cocoa powder can be applied to a glass for Brandy Alexander, Cara Sposa or any other creamy cocktail flavoured with chocolate, coffee or orange.

To frost a glass, tip the rim of the glass in water, egg white, citrus juice or one of the syrups, and then dip it again in the chosen frosting. The garnish will take on the colour of the liquid.

Citrus fruits

Edible garnishes should reflect the various contents of the cocktail. Citrus fruit is widely used because it is appetizing to look at, and can be cut in advance and kept covered in the refrigerator for a day until needed. Whole slices cut halfway through can be balanced on the rim of a highball glass, while half-slices are best used for floating in a cocktail glass. Apple, pear and banana are also suitable, but they do discolour on exposure to the air; dip them in lemon juice first to preserve colour and flavour.

Lemon is probably the most important fruit of all for the bartender. It is handy in everything from a simple gin and tonic to almost any cocktail.

A lime is small enough for you to be able to use whole slices to garnish a sharp-tasting cocktail containing its juice, such as a Moscow Mule.

Orange is indispensable for garnishing not just orange-flavoured drinks, but old-time mixtures of vermouth and spirit, such as Negroni.

Kumquats are bitter little citrus fruits, which are eaten with the skin on. Use half of one on a stick to garnish a cocktail that has some bitter orange flavour in it.

Above: Oranges.

Left: Kumquats.

Left: Limes.

Left: Lemons.

USING CITRUS FRUITS

A twisted half-slice of lemon adds an elegant decoration to any cocktail containing lemon juice.

A simple twist of lime looks effective and adds to the taste of a tequila, banana and lime cocktail.

Grated orange rind goes well with drinks containing orange, such as this creamy chocolatey-orange Tuaca and orange curaçao cocktail.

Soft fruits

Fresh soft fruit such as strawberries, cherries, peaches, apricots, blackberries and redcurrants make fabulous splashes of colour and add a delicious flavour, although they still tend to be mainly available in the summer.

Quartered large strawberries or, better still, the whole, small, wild variety, such as the French *fraises des bois*, would look good on a Strawberry Kiss.

Whole fresh cherries, particularly the black varieties, can be used in place of standard cocktail cherries from a jar to adorn a drink containing cherry brandy

or kirsch. Singapore Sling contains the former, Rose the latter. The maraschino cherry is a popular option too, even though it is seen as something of a cliché these days.

A thin slice of very ripe peach is appropriate for a drink containing peach schnapps or peach brandy, such as Sparkling Peach Melba. White peach is best.

If there's apricot brandy in the drink (for example, Festival), a thin slice of apricot will work well. Use only juicy-ripe fruits though. The French Bergeron is a good variety.

Blackberries are the only garnish to use for a Blackberry and Champagne Crush, so long as they're in season.

The endless supply of tropical fruits available all year long, such as mango, pineapple, star fruit, papaya, physalis and the various types of melon, offers numerous decorative ideas and combinations for garnishing. A twiglet of redcurrants, perhaps with a little sugar frosting, makes a rather Christmassy-looking garnish. Physalis is a favourite garnish for modern desserts. Bring it into the cocktail repertoire too for exotically flavoured drinks.

Below: Cherries.

Below: Strawberries.

Left: Apricots.

Above: Peaches.

Below: Blackberries.

USING SOFT FRUITS

A cherry and an apricot slice can be skewered with a cocktail stick to make a stylish, fruity garnish.

Below: Physalis.

Above: Redcurrants.

*Above:
Chocolate.*

Above: Nutmeg.

Above: Green and black olives.

Above: Red chillies.

Below: Cherry tomatoes.

*Right:
Mint.*

Above: Celery.

Other garnishes

Not all garnishes and decorations need be fruit, however. A block of chocolate can be grated over a drink, or melted and scraped into chocolate curls, to decorate a cocktail such as Iced Mint and Chocolate Cooler.

Ground (or whole) cinnamon makes an appropriate garnish for hot mulled wine or punch.

Nutmeg goes well with egg-nogs and flips. Either grate whole nutmegs, or add the powdered version to the surface of cream cocktails containing chocolate or coffee flavours. A Brandy Alexander cries out for nutmeg.

To some, green olives are indispensable in a Dry Martini; to others, they are anathema. When Martinis do call for a green olive, always opt for those packaged in brine, not in oil.

Plain or chilli-pepper vodka can stand up to pickled chillies, while the Martini variant known as a Gibson would not be a Gibson without a white pearl onion.

Red chillies should certainly set the palate alight in a drink already containing pepper vodka.

Cherry tomatoes are an interesting alternative for garnishing a Bloody Mary, while celery is the Bloody Mary's very own swizzle-stick.

As well as forming an integral ingredient in some cocktails, a sprig of fresh mint makes an appealing garnish, perhaps to the creamy, mint-flavoured Grasshopper.

A sprig of fresh mint adds freshness to drinks such as this Long Island Iced Tea, or anything containing crème de menthe.

Grated dark chocolate adds flavour to sweet cocktails such as this gin, banana and cream mixture.

Whole cinnamon sticks can be used as stirrers for hot drinks such as coffee or hot chocolate.

Tricks and techniques of the trade

It is worth mastering the techniques for the preparation of good-looking drinks. The following pages give you precise directions for some of the essential procedures, such as crushing ice, as well as some not-so-essential skills, such as making decorative ice cubes. Mastering these tricks of the trade is what will distinguish the dedicated bartender from the amateur dabbler.

Crushing ice

Some cocktails require cracked or crushed ice for adding to glasses, or a finely crushed ice "snow" for blending. It isn't a good idea to break ice up in a blender or food processor as you may find it damages the blades. Instead:

1 Lay out a cloth, such as a clean glass cloth or dishtowel, on a work surface, and cover half of it with ice cubes. (If you wish, you can also use a cloth ice bag.)

2 Fold the cloth over and, using the end of a rolling pin, or better still a wooden mallet of the sort used for tenderizing meat, smash down on the ice firmly several times, until you achieve the required fineness.

3 Spoon the ice into glasses or a pitcher. Fine ice snow must be used immediately because it melts away like morning mist, but cracked or roughly crushed ice can be stored in the freezer in plastic bags. Stay up all night with a sledgehammer, and you should have enough to do a moderate-sized social gathering. Alternatively, just buy an ice crusher.

Making decorative ice cubes

Decorative ice cubes can instantly jolly up the simplest of cocktails. Flavour and colour the water with fruit juices or bitters, and freeze in three stages.

1 Half-fill each compartment of an ice cube tray with water and place in the freezer for 2–3 hours, or until the water has frozen.

2 Prepare the fruit, olives, mint leaves, lemon rind, raisins or borage flowers and dip each briefly in water. Place in the ice-cube trays, put in the freezer and freeze again.

3 Top up the ice-cube trays with water and return to the freezer to freeze completely. Use as required, but only in one drink at each session.

Frosting glasses

The appearance and taste of a cocktail are enhanced if the rims of the glasses are frosted. Use celery salt, grated coconut, grated chocolate, coloured sugars or cocoa for an eye-catching effect. Once it is frosted, place the glass in the refrigerator to chill until needed, if you have time.

1 Hold the glass upside down, so the juice does not run down the glass. Rub the rim of the glass with the cut surface of a lemon, lime, orange or even a slice of fresh pineapple.

2 Keeping the glass upside down, dip the rim into a shallow layer of sugar, coconut or salt. Redip the glass, if necessary, and turn it so that the rim is well-coated.

3 Stand the glass upright and let it sit until the sugar, coconut or salt has dried on the rim, then chill.

Bartending know-how
Instead of using fruit juice as the frosting liquid, you can rub a glass rim with egg white instead.

Shaking cocktails

Cocktails that contain sugar syrups or creams require more than just a stir; they are combined and chilled with a brief shake. Remember that it is possible to shake only one or two servings at once, so you may have to work quickly in batches. Always use fresh ice each time.

1 Add four or five ice cubes to the shaker and pour in all the ingredients.

2 Put the lid on the shaker. Hold the shaker firmly in one hand, keeping the lid in place with the other hand.

3 Shake vigorously for about 15 seconds to blend simple concoctions, and for 20–30 seconds for drinks with sugar syrups, cream or egg. By this time, the shaker should feel extremely cold.

4 Remove the small cap and pour into the prepared glass, using a strainer if the shaker is not already fitted with one.

Bartending know-how
Never shake anything sparkling, whether lemonade or best champagne. It will flatten it.

Making twists

As an alternative to slices of the fruit, many drinks are garnished with a twist of orange, lemon or lime rind. The most famous one is Horse's Neck, but twists are useful in many other recipes. They should be made before the drink itself is prepared, so that you don't keep a cold cocktail waiting. Here's how:

1 Choose a fruit with an unblemished skin and a regular shape.

2 Using a canelle knife or potato peeler, start at the tip of the fruit and start peeling round, as though you were peeling an apple.

3 Work slowly and carefully down the fruit, being sure to keep the pared-away rind in one continuous strip.

4 Trim it, if necessary, to a length that suits the glass.

Melon balling

A gadget exists for producing perfect little balls of melon that can be used to decorate a cocktail.

1 Cut the ripe melon in half, and scoop out the seeds with a dessert spoon.

2 Push the baller deeply into the flesh of the fruit, and then turn it through 360° to extract as near to a perfect sphere as you can.

3 Thread balls of different-coloured melon (e.g. Galia, Charentais and watermelon) on to a cocktail stick for full visual impact.

Bartending know-how
Choose ripe melon by its fully developed skin colour, which should be properly deep.

Muddling

A muddler – a long stick with a bulbous end – is the only thing to use for pressing the juice out of mint leaves for use in cocktails in which the mint is an ingredient, rather than just a garnish.

Flaming sugar for absinthe

This technique of adding sugar to your absinthe is favoured by the Czechs. It is more dramatic than simply pouring water over it in the Parisian fashion, and is more efficient anyway.

Making basic sugar syrup

A sugar syrup is sometimes preferable to dry sugar for sweetening cocktails, since it blends immediately with the other ingredients. This recipe makes about 750ml/1¼ pints.

350g/12oz sugar
60cl/1 pint water

1 Place the sugar in a heavy pan with the water, and heat gently over a low heat. Stir the mixture with a wooden spoon until all of the sugar has dissolved completely.

1 Put the mint leaves and caster (superfine) sugar or sugar syrup in the bottom of your glass.

1 Put a sugar cube on a perforated spoon and immerse it in a generous shot of absinthe until it is saturated.

2 Give the leaves an initial twist and turn to break them up and mix them into the sugar.

2 Balancing the spoon across the top of the glass, use a match to set fire to the sugar cube.

2 Brush the sides of the pan with a pastry brush dampened in water, to remove any sugar crystals that might cause the syrup to crystallize.

3 Press them forcefully, with repeated turns of the wrist, to extract their juices.

3 As the sugar cooks, the flame will gradually die down, and when it does, gently lower the melting cube once more into the drink, and stir it in to dissolve it.

4 Add the same quantity of cold water as absinthe, and stir the drink once more. It's all a bit of a fuss, but worth it.

3 Bring to the boil for 3–5 minutes. Skim any scum away and when no more appears, remove the pan from the heat. Cool and pour into clean, dry, airtight bottles. Keep in the refrigerator for up to one month.

Bartending know-how

Muddling is a vigorous process that involves more force than any other technique, apart from ice-smashing.

Bartending know-how

Homemade sugar syrup is a useful standby ingredient, and cheaper than buying sirop de gomme.

Making flavoured syrup

Syrup can be flavoured with anything: a split vanilla pod, mint leaves or citrus rind. Simply boil, and then bottle with the syrup. This recipe makes about 450ml/¾ pint syrup.

900g/2lb very ripe soft or stone fruit, washed
350g/12oz sugar

1 Put the washed fruit of your choice in a bowl and, using the bottom of a rolling pin, a wooden pestle or a potato masher, crush the fruit to release the juices.

2 Cover and allow to sit overnight to concentrate the flavour.

3 Strain the purée through a cloth bag or piece of muslin (cheesecloth). Gather the corners of the cloth together and twist them tight, to remove as much juice as possible.

4 Measure the amount of juice and add 225g/8oz sugar to every 300ml/½ pint fruit juice.

5 Place the pan on a low heat, and gently stir until all the sugar has dissolved. Continue as for basic sugar syrup. The syrup will keep in the refrigerator for up to one month.

Making flavoured spirits

Gin, vodka and white rum can be left to steep and absorb the flavours of a wide variety of soft fruits. This recipe makes about 1.2 litres/2 pints.

450g/1lb raspberries, strawberries, or pineapple
225g/8oz sugar
1 litre/1¾ pints gin, vodka or light rum

1 Put the fruit in a wide-necked jar, and add the sugar.

2 Add the spirit. Cover tightly. Leave in a cool, dark place for a month, shaking gently every week.

3 Strain through clean muslin (cheesecloth) or a cloth bag, and squeeze out the rest of the liquid from the steeped fruit. Return the flavoured liquor to a clean bottle and seal. Store in a cool, dark place. It will happily keep for a year.

Steeping spirits

The process of steeping any spirit with a flavouring agent, such as chillies, creates a whole new sensation. This recipe makes about 1 litre/1¾ pints.

25–50g/1–2oz small red chillies, or to taste, washed
1 litre/1¾ pints sherry or vodka

1 Using a cocktail stick, prick the chillies all over to release their flavours.

2 Pack the chillies tightly into a sterilized bottle.

3 Top up with sherry or vodka. Fit the cork tightly and leave in a dark place for at least ten days or up to two months.

Variations

Try the following interesting alternatives: gin with cumin seeds, star anise or juniper berries; brandy with 25g/1oz peeled and sliced fresh ginger, or 15g/½oz whole cloves; vodka with 50g/2oz washed raisins, or 15–30ml/1–2 tbsp cracked black peppercorns; rum with 2–3 pricked vanilla pods. The amount of flavouring used is of course a matter of personal taste.

Planning a party

The key to planning and carrying out your first successful cocktail party is to start small. Inviting the entire neighbourhood to a riotous bash might sound rather tempting, but you will only come unstuck by overreaching your own resources. A small group of old friends – say, half a dozen – is a good starting point.

Browse through the third part of this book, try out for yourself a few of the recipes that appeal to you, and whittle them down to two or three that you think will prove popular with guests whose tastes are familiar to you. A pleasing balance of sour and sweet, or sour, sweet and fizzy, drinks will make for a satisfying evening. Choosing one cocktail that can be made in the liquidizer, one that is made in the shaker and one that is mixed in a pitcher would make logistical sense, so that you are not frantically rinsing out the shaker as guests move from one cocktail to another.

State your start and end times in advance when you invite people. That way, you can ensure that you are not still dealing with thirsty stragglers at one o'clock in the morning.

Provide food, but make it clear that this is a cocktail evening, not a dinner

Below: Champagne chilling in a bucket of iced water needs about 15 minutes.

Above: Nibbles will help absorb some of the alcohol consumed.

party. You are going to be quite busy enough with drink preparation, without having to cook. However, the more guests are encouraged to eat, the slower the intoxication effect will set in. Little salty and cheesy nibbles, tortilla chips with dips, and nuts are always popular. If you really want to splash out, you could make or buy some canapés ahead of time as well.

Decide on which glasses you are going to use for which cocktail, and make sure there is one of each for each guest. Go through your checklist of vital equipment several times, to be certain you haven't forgotten anything: shaker (with measures), liquidizer, pitcher, glasses, fruit for garnishing (remember that citrus fruit slices and twists can be prepared in advance before anyone arrives), a knife for last-minute slicing, bags of ice, and any special opening implements for flipping off bottle-tops or pulling corks. Serving each drink on a little folded paper napkin is the kind of touch that really impresses.

Quantities will depend on how many people you invite, but it is worth doing some initial calculations. A standard measure in these recipes is 25ml/1fl oz,

of which there are 28 in a standard bottle of spirits and 20 in a 50cl bottle of liqueur. Divide each bottle not by single measures, but by the number of measures in each recipe, which may be higher or lower than one. For some drinks, you may find a half-bottle will be quite enough to be going on with.

If there is one golden rule, it has to be that you can never have too much ice. Cocktail-making uses an enormous amount, as each batch is used for the few seconds it takes you to shake the cocktail, and is then thrown away. But ice is only water after all, so be extravagant, and if you aren't sure you have enough ice trays or bags to cope, then buy one of those industrial-sized bags of ice from the supermarket. Better still, buy two or three, which shouldn't set you back too much. They aren't very cost-effective, I admit, but at some late stage in the evening, you'll be mighty glad it's there, if only to clamp firmly on your head as you see the last happy guests away.

So good luck, and have fun!

Alcohol and health

It has now been established that one glass of wine a day could be good for you. It is a bulwark in the body's defence against coronary heart disease because its antioxidants help to break down bad cholesterol in the arteries. To some extent, ethanol (alcohol) itself in any of its forms can assist in this, as has been found by scientists in Denmark, but there are obviously limits. Alcohol is virtually worthless in terms of nutritional value and, if drunk in excess, is positively harmful.

Heavy drinking damages the liver, possibly irreparably, and puts strain on its normal day-to-day functioning. It also depletes nutrients, such as vitamins A and C, the B vitamins, magnesium, zinc and the essential fatty acids, and leads to severe dehydration.

Modern methods of producing alcoholic drinks often mean that your average glass of wine, beer or spirit will contain chemical pesticides, colourants

Below: Nuts and fruits are efficient sources of protein and vitamins to replace essential nutrients.

and other noxious additives, which you might be a lot more circumspect about if you found them in food products.

Each drinker famously has his or her own limit. What may be no more than a convivial evening's imbibing to one would have the next person sliding under the table. As a very general rule, an adult woman's capacity is thought to be about two-thirds that of a man's, so women shouldn't feel under any pressure to keep pace.

It would be disingenuous to pretend that you won't at some stage wake up feeling so unutterably lousy that you'll swear to forgo all strong liquors forever more. Welcome to the wonderful world of the alcohol hangover, caused by dehydration and too much toxin in the bloodstream. Everybody has his or her own best cure, whether it be milk, fried foods, black coffee, the rather dubious hair-of-the-dog approach (i.e. another small drink) or my own indispensable standby: aspirin.

Far smarter than a hangover cure, though, is knowing how to avoid such a ghastly outcome in the first place. Ways

Above: Fruit juices will help to make life fun during periods of abstinence.

of doing this include: lining the stomach with lactic fat (300ml/½ pint whole milk) before you embark on the evening's drinking; taking 500mg of aspirin beforehand; downing a glass of water between drinks to rehydrate; and (most important of all) slowly drinking a pint of water before falling into bed.

Treat yourself to a break from it all periodically. Non-alcoholic juices made from fruits and vegetables stimulate the body, speed up metabolism, encourage the elimination of toxins via the lymphatic system, and strengthen the body's overall immunity. They play a vital role in detoxing – everyone's favourite pastime in January – and should be drunk fresh. When making juices at home, choose ripe fruits and vegetables. Fresh juices can be very strong, so dilute with filtered or mineral water to taste. They should always be drunk as soon as they are made.

Health-food stores and pharmacies sell a natural remedy called milk thistle in capsule form, which has been clinically proven to assist in liver cell regeneration. Take it in doses of up to 200mg per day, especially during periods of abstinence. It really will make you feel better.

Making drinks

Now we can get down to business. The recipes in
this part of the book are a mixture of old formulas
that go back to the America of the 19th century;
cocktails from the great jazz era of the 1920s;
drinks that came to prominence in the cocktail
revival of the 1980s; and new ones being drunk in
trendsetting bars today. They are grouped into
their basic drink categories in the same order that
we encountered them in the first part of the book.
For all recipes, 1 measure should be taken as the
standard cocktail measure, that is 25ml or 1fl oz.
A "dash" is the amount that escapes from the
bottle by tilting it and righting it again over
the shaker in about half a second. Where orange,
lemon and lime juices are specified, they should
ideally be from the freshly squeezed fruit.

Gin

Of the six basic spirits that are used in cocktail-making, gin is the most versatile. That may seem strange in view of its assertively perfumed character, but it is precisely the herb and spice aromatics in its composition that enable it to blend well with a range of liqueurs and fruit juices, and even other spirits. In addition to that, it has in common with plain vodka, white rum and silver tequila the useful attribute of colourlessness, so that it makes a neutral background for some flamboyant-looking creations. Use a good brand of London gin in these recipes, except where one of the other types, such as Plymouth or Dutch genever, is specifically called for.

As with each section in this part of the book, we shall begin with the old classic recipes, which tend to do no more than slightly modify the flavour of the essential ingredient, before progressing on through the ages to today's more complex and challenging mixtures.

Gin Fizz

The combination of sourness and fizziness in this 19th-century recipe is what makes it so refreshing.

2 measures/3 tbsp gin
juice of half a large lemon
5ml/1 tsp caster (superfine) sugar
soda water

Shake the gin, lemon juice and sugar with ice until the sugar is properly dissolved. Pour out into a frosted, tall, narrow glass half-filled with ice, and top up with soda. Add two straws. There should ideally be a little less soda than the other combined ingredients, but it is very much a matter of personal taste.

Tom Collins

This is similar to a Gin Fizz, except that it isn't shaken and tends to be made with a little less soda. Originally known as John Collins, after the head waiter at a London hotel in the early 19th century, it changed its name when it began to made with the Old Tom brand of gin.

2 measures/3 tbsp gin
juice of half a large lemon
5ml/1 tsp sugar
soda water

Pour the gin and lemon juice into a frosted, tall glass half-filled with ice. Add the sugar and stir to dissolve. Add roughly a measure and a half of soda, a slice of lemon and a couple of straws.

Gin Swizzle

The Swizzle dates from the early 19th century, and was originally a drink made frothy purely by energetic stirring. The implement used for this, the swizzle-stick, took its name from the drink.

2 measures/3 tbsp gin
¼ measure/1 tsp sugar syrup
juice of a lime
2 dashes Angostura bitters

Beat all the ingredients together (as if you were preparing eggs for an omelette) in a large jug, with ice. When the drink is good and foaming, strain it into a tall glass. Alternatively, make the drink in the tall glass, but remember to stir it up vigorously with a swizzle-stick. Some recipes add soda water to achieve the swizzle effect, but originally it was all done by elbow grease. The froth will subside fairly quickly anyway.

Bartending know-how
The invention of gin is apocryphally credited to one Franciscus de la Boë, a medical professor at the University of Leiden in the Netherlands, sometime in the mid-17th century. Even if he is the true progenitor of gin, however, he was almost certainly not the first to add juniper berries for medicinal reasons to a pure distilled spirit. The 12th-century monastery at Salerno, where European distillation was born, is the most likely origin of the basic recipe.

Gin Sling

Precursor of the Fizz, the Sling started life in the mid-18th century as a mixture of gin, lemon juice and sugar, but used plain water instead of sparkling. In later times, it also came to have a bittering element added to the sour, as here.

2 measures/3 tbsp gin
juice of half a lemon
5ml/1 tsp sugar
dash of Angostura bitters
still mineral water

Mix the gin, lemon juice, sugar and Angostura in a tumbler with plenty of ice until the sugar is fully dissolved. Top up the glass with cold water straight from the refrigerator. Add a twist of lemon rind and straws.

Gin Cocktail

A very simple preparation of fruity, bittered gin, this makes a highly sophisticated aperitif.

2 measures/3 tbsp gin
5 dashes orange bitters

Shake the ingredients well with ice and strain into a cocktail glass. This is one of those drinks that needs no garnish, but is perfect just as it is.

Gin Sour

The Sour dates from the 1850s, and can be made with any of the basic spirits. Fresh lemon juice is naturally the key to it, with the edge taken off it by means of a pinch of sugar. However, it should never taste at all sweet, otherwise it wouldn't be worthy of its name.

2 measures/3 tbsp gin
juice of half a large lemon
5ml/1 tsp caster (superfine) sugar

Shake all the ingredients together with ice and strain into a rocks glass or small tumbler. Some bartenders add the briefest squirt of soda just before serving for extra pep, but it is better served wholly still.

Dry Martini

No cocktail recipe is more energetically argued over than the classic dry Martini. It is basically a generous measure of virtually neat, stone-cold gin with a dash of dry white vermouth in it. But how much is a dash? Purists insist on no more than a single drop, or the residue left after briefly flushing the glass out with a splash of vermouth and then pouring it away. (They puzzlingly refer to such a Martini as "very dry", as if adding more vermouth would sweeten it. In fact, the terminology

Orange Blossom

The original gin and orange, much drunk during the Prohibition era in the United States, where the fruit juice masked the ghastly flavour of bathtub gin. Note that the spirit isn't drowned with too much juice. Some recipes add a pinch of sugar, but it doesn't need it.

1½ measures/6 tsp gin
1½ measures/6 tsp freshly squeezed
    orange juice

Shake the ingredients with ice, and strain into a cocktail glass.

harks back to the original recipe, when the vermouth used was the sweet red variety.) Some go for as much as half a measure of vermouth, which is guaranteed to send the purist into paroxysms of horror. If in doubt, it makes more sense to incline towards the purist philosophy: the vermouth should be added as if it were the last bottle in existence. Inevitably, individual preference remains the crucial factor.

The drink should properly be mixed gently in a large pitcher, with ice, and then strained into the traditional cocktail glass (the real name of which is a Martini glass), which should be straight out of the freezer. A twist of lemon rind should be squeezed delicately over the surface, so that the essential oil floats in globules on top of the drink, but don't put the lemon twist in the glass. The addition of a green olive to the glass is traditional, but definitely disliked by some for its salty pungency.

Clover Club

A traditional recipe from the 1920s cocktail era, named after a celebrated nightclub in Chicago.

2 measures/3 tbsp gin
juice of half a large lemon
1 measure/1½ tbsp grenadine
1 egg white

Shake all the ingredients with ice for at least 30 seconds to make sure the egg white is thoroughly incorporated. Strain into a rocks glass, and garnish with a half-slice of lemon.

Gibson

Well loved in Japan, this version of the Martini is named after one Charles Gibson, an American illustrator who found a cocktail onion in the drink more to his taste than the traditional olive. You can afford to be a little more generous with the vermouth.

½ measure/2 tsp dry white vermouth
2½ measures/3½ tbsp gin
2 cocktail onions

Pour the vermouth and gin into a large glass or pitcher with plenty of ice, and stir for at least 30 seconds to chill well. Strain into a Martini glass. Skewer the onions on to the end of a cocktail stick and add to the glass, so that they sit temptingly at the bottom. Better still, pour out the drink over the onions to release their flavours.

Gimlet

Like the Sour, the Gimlet is a small, sharply flavoured drink, but it is made with lime rather than lemon. As fresh lime juice is exceptionally sour, lime cordial is used, which is classically Rose's, as this was once the only brand available. The gin should ideally be Plymouth. The 1930 recipe in the *Savoy Cocktail Book* uses half-and-half proportions, but these days it is better adjusted to the quantities below so as not to be too syrupy. Some bartenders add a touch of soda.

2 measures/3 tbsp Plymouth gin
¾ measure/3 tsp Rose's lime cordial

Shake both ingredients well with ice and strain into a cocktail glass.

Bitter Gimlet

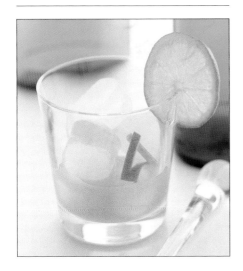

This is an old-fashioned aperitif, which could easily be turned into a longer drink by finishing it with chilled tonic or soda water.

1 lime, cut into wedges
1 measure/1½ tbsp gin
2 dashes Angostura bitters

Put the lime into a pitcher and, using a muddler, press the juice out of it. Add the cracked ice, gin and bitters and stir well until chilled. Strain the cocktail into a short tumbler over ice cubes. Add a triangle of lime rind to the drink.

Horse's Neck

The name derives from the shape of the lemon rind that hangs in the glass. There are various versions of this mix, the earliest using bourbon or brandy, but gin eventually became the most popular.

1 lemon
2 measures/3 tbsp gin
dry ginger ale

My Fair Lady

This frothy, fruity cocktail was invented at London's Savoy Hotel in the 1950s to coincide with a production of the much-loved Lerner and Loewe musical based on George Bernard Shaw's play *Pygmalion*.

1 measure/1½ tbsp gin
½ measure/2 tsp orange juice
½ measure/2 tsp lemon juice
¼ measure/1 tsp crème de fraise
1 egg white

Cut the entire rind from a lemon, spiral-fashion, as in the recipe for Gin Crusta. Dangle it from the rim of a tall glass so that it hangs down inside. Add plenty of cracked ice and the gin, and then top up with ginger ale. You can also add a dash of Angostura bitters if the mood takes you, but it is by no means essential.

Shake all the ingredients thoroughly with ice, and strain into a cocktail glass.

Gin and Lemon Fizz

If gin and tonic is your tipple, try this chilled alternative. The fruit and flower ice cubes make a lively decoration for any iced drink. This recipe serves two.

mixture of small edible berries or currants
pieces of thinly pared lemon or orange rind
tiny edible flowers
4 scoops of lemon sorbet
30ml/2 tbsp gin
120ml/4fl oz chilled tonic water

To make the decorated ice cubes, place each fruit, piece of rind or flower in a section of an ice-cube tray. Carefully fill with water and freeze for several hours until the cubes are solid. Divide the sorbet into two cocktail glasses or use small tumblers, with a capacity of about 150ml/¼ pint. Spoon over the gin and add a couple of the ornamental ice cubes to each glass. Top up with tonic water and serve immediately.

Bartending know-how
When making the ice cubes, choose small herb flowers such as borage or mint, or edible flowers such as rose geraniums, primulas or rose buds.

Gin Cobbler

The Cobbler is a very early drink, American in origin, that was served in the summer. It is basically sweetened spirit lavishly decorated with fruit. Brandy, whisky and dry sherry make popular alternatives to the gin version described here.

5ml/1 tsp caster (superfine) sugar
2 measures/3 tbsp gin
soda water
fruit, to garnish

Dissolve the sugar in a little water in a large goblet. Half-fill the glass with cracked ice and add the gin. Stir well and then double the quantity of liquid with soda water. The drink should then be adorned with slices of orange, lemon, pineapple, or whatever comes to hand, and drunk through straws.

White Lady

This is one of the classic cocktail recipes of the 1920s, and is still going strong today. The high strength of the alcohol ingredients and the sharpness of the lemon quite belie its innocuous reputation as a "lady's drink".

1 measure/1½ tbsp gin
1 measure/1½ tbsp Cointreau
1 measure/1½ tbsp lemon juice

Shake the ingredients with ice and strain into a frosted cocktail glass. Some recipes also add 5ml/1 tsp egg white. The *Savoy Cocktail Book* makes no mention of it. It simply gives the drink a frothier texture, if that's what you like. Garnish with a lime twist.

Perfect Lady

A blended cocktail with a nice sharp edge, given a frothy texture with a little egg white.

1 measure/1½ tbsp gin
½ measure/2 tsp peach brandy
½ measure/2 tsp lemon juice
1 measure/1½ tbsp egg white

Put all the ingredients into a liquidizer with a good handful of crushed ice, blend for a few seconds, and then pour into a champagne bowl. Garnish with a slice of juicy fresh peach.

Bartending know-how
When using eggs, always be sure that they are very fresh. The whites will whip better in this condition.

Tod's Cooler

The name of this cocktail refers to Tod Sloan, an American jockey of the era before the First World War, who invented this drink at one of his favourite haunts, the bar of the Palace Hotel in Brussels. Known to English racegoers as Toddy, his more famous nickname, coined in the States, was Yankee Doodle Dandy.

2 measures/3 tbsp gin
⅔ measure/1 tbsp crème de cassis
⅔ measure/1 tbsp lemon juice
soda water

Half-fill a tall glass with cracked ice, add the first three ingredients and then top up with soda. Garnish with a spiral twist of lemon rind.

Gin Smash

Try this cocktail with any fresh mint you can find: peppermint and spearmint would each contribute their own flavour to this simple and very refreshing summery drink.

15ml/1 tbsp sugar
4 sprigs fresh mint
2 measures/3 tbsp gin

Dissolve the sugar in a little water in the cocktail shaker. Add the mint and, using a muddler, bruise and press the juices out of the leaves. Then add plenty of crushed ice, and finally the gin. Shake for about 20 seconds. Strain into a small wine glass filled with crushed ice. If desired, add fresh mint sprigs and drinking straws.

Leap Year

The particular year in question was 1928, when Harry Craddock, a barman at the Savoy Hotel in London, created this drink for a party held there on February 29.

2 measures/3 tbsp gin
½ measure/2 tsp Grand Marnier
½ measure/2 tsp sweet red vermouth
dash lemon juice, plus lemon rind

Shake well and strain into a cocktail glass. Squeeze a bit of lemon rind over the surface of the drink so that a little of its oil sprays out.

Gin Rickey

The Rickey was invented in the last decade of the 19th century in the United States. It is almost the same as a Gimlet, only without the sweetening element of the cordial, which makes it a much more acerbic proposition. It can be made with any spirit, although gin is the original version.

juice and rind of half a lime
2 measures/3 tbsp gin
soda water

Half-fill a tall glass with ice. Squeeze the lime directly into the glass and then drop in the empty rind. Add the gin and stir vigorously, before topping with soda.

Gin Crusta

Prepare the glass in advance and keep it chilled in the refrigerator ready for instant use. The depth of pink colour will depend on the strength of the maraschino cherry juice you use.

1 lemon
25g/2 tbsp golden granulated sugar
3 dashes sugar syrup
2 dashes maraschino cherry juice
2 dashes Angostura bitters
1 measure/1½ tbsp gin

Cut both ends off the lemon and, using a canelle knife, peel it thinly in one long, continuous piece. Halve the lemon and rub the rim of a glass with the cut surface. Dip it into the sugar to create a decorative rim. Arrange the lemon rind in a scroll on the inside of a high-sided glass. Add the sugar syrup, cherry juice, Angostura, gin and juice of a quarter of the lemon to a cocktail shaker, half-filled with ice. Shake well and strain into the prepared glass.

Monkey Gland

From the classic cocktail era of the early 1920s, this drink was created at Ciro's Club in London, a legendary jazz nightspot just off the Charing Cross Road. Head bartender Harry McElhone later moved to Paris to run Harry's New York Bar, where he ascended to true international renown.

2 measures/3 tbsp gin
1 measure/1½ tbsp orange juice
½ measure/2 tsp grenadine
½ measure/2 tsp absinthe

Shake the ingredients with plenty of ice, and strain into a large wine glass. Garnish with a slice of orange.

Amsterdam

This deliciously orangey cocktail is unusual in having the ice left in it. It was invented in the city whose name it bears. Squeeze a fresh mandarin if you have one, or else use unsweetened juice from a can of mandarin segments.

1½ measures/6 tsp gin
½ measure/2 tsp Cointreau
¾ measure/3 tsp mandarin juice
1–2 mandarin segments

Shake the gin, Cointreau and mandarin juice with cracked ice and pour, without straining, into a rocks glass. Add a mandarin segment or two.

Lady Killer

A lusciously fruity, tropical-flavoured cocktail from a bar called the Wantagh Arms in New York State. It would make a good summer's afternoon cocktail.

1 measure/1½ tbsp gin
¾ measure/3 tsp apricot brandy
¾ measure/3 tsp Cointreau
2 measures/3 tbsp passion fruit juice
2 measures/3 tbsp pineapple juice

Shake all the ingredients together with ice, and strain into a highball glass half-filled with cracked ice. Garnish with a wedge of pineapple.

Pink Pussycat

An object-lesson in how easily gin takes to a range of tangy fruit flavours in a mixed drink, Pink Pussycat also has – as its name suggests – a most beguiling colour.

2 measures/3 tbsp gin
3 measures/4½ tbsp pineapple juice
2 measures/3 tbsp grapefruit juice
½ measure/2 tsp grenadine

Shake all the ingredients well with ice, and strain into a tall glass. Garnish with a segment of grapefruit.

Wilga Hill Boomerang

This sundowner is mixed in a large pitcher half-filled with ice cubes, and is served extremely cold.

1 measure/1½ tbsp gin
¼ measure/1 tsp dry vermouth
¼ measure/1 tsp sweet red vermouth
1 measure/1½ tbsp apple juice
dash Angostura bitters
2 dashes maraschino cherry juice

Pour the gin, dry and sweet vermouths and apple juice into a pitcher half-filled with cracked ice, and stir until the outside of the glass has frosted. Add the Angostura bitters and cherry juice to the bottom of a cocktail glass and add crushed ice, and then strain in the mixed cocktail. Prepare a strip of orange rind and a maraschino cherry to decorate the glass.

Arctic Summer

This is a very appealing, sunset-coloured cocktail. Don't stint on the ice.

1½ measures/6 tsp gin
¾ measure/3 tsp apricot brandy
¼ measure/1 tsp grenadine
4 measures/6 tbsp sparkling bitter lemon

Fill a highball glass with cracked ice, and add the ingredients one by one in the order above. Do not stir. Garnish with a slice of lemon and a cocktail cherry.

Vunderful

A long, lazy Sunday afternoon tipple, conjured up in the heat of southern Africa. Leave the fruits in the gin for as long as possible. This recipe contains 20 servings.

400g/14oz can lychees
2 peaches, sliced
¾ bottle gin

For each serving you will need:
1 measure/1½ tbsp Pimm's
2–3 dashes Angostura bitters
5 measures/120ml/4fl oz chilled tonic water
  or lemonade

Strain the lychees from the syrup and place them in a wide-necked jar with the peach slices and the gin. Let them sit overnight or for anything up to a month. For each serving, mix in a large pitcher a measure of the lychee gin with the Pimm's and the bitters to taste. Strain into tall tumblers filled with ice cubes. Add chilled tonic water or lemonade to top up. Put a couple of the drained gin-soaked lychees and peach slices into each glass, stirring and crushing the fruit into the drink with a muddler. Add a half-slice of lime to the rim of each glass.

Luigi

A 1920s classic, Luigi was created at the Criterion restaurant on London's Piccadilly Circus by one Luigi Naintré.

1½ measures/6 tsp gin
1½ measures/6 tsp dry vermouth
¼ measure/1 tsp grenadine
dash Cointreau
juice of half a tangerine or mandarin orange

Shake well with ice and strain into a glass. Add a segment of tangerine.

Bartending know-how
Mandarins and tangerines taste much the same, but the latter are full of pips.

Pink Lady

Yet another of the "Ladies", this one is more venerable than most. It dates from before the First World War, and was named after a now forgotten, hit stage play. The pink colour is achieved by means of a relatively large quantity of the pomegranite syrup, grenadine.

caster (superfine) sugar, for frosting
1½ measures/6 tsp Plymouth gin
½ measure/2 tsp grenadine, plus extra for frosting
½ measure/2 tsp double (heavy) cream
¼ measure/1 tsp lemon juice
1 measure/1½ tbsp egg white

Dip the rim of a champagne saucer or bowl-shaped cocktail glass into grenadine and then into caster sugar to create a bright pink, frosted rim. Shake the cocktail ingredients with ice and strain into the prepared glass. Garnish with a cherry.

Mistress

This is a long, delicately creamy cocktail. The Campari topping just gives it a tantalizing edge of bitterness.

1½ measures/6 tsp gin
1 measure/1½ tbsp white crème de cacao
2 measures/3 tbsp pineapple juice
1 measure/1½ tbsp passion fruit juice
1 measure/1½ tbsp whipping cream
¼ measure/1 tsp Campari

Shake all the ingredients except the last with ice, and then strain into a highball glass, half-filled with ice cubes. Drizzle the Campari on top.

Mayfair

Also dating from the 1920s, Mayfair was invented at the Embassy Club in that district of London. The recipe calls for syrup of cloves, which you may have difficulty tracking down, but its flavour is quite inimitable if you can. It has a sweetly floral quality.

1½ measures/6 tsp gin
¾ measure/3 tsp apricot brandy
¾ measure/3 tsp orange juice
¼ measure/1 tsp clove syrup

Shake all the ingredients well with ice, and strain into a cocktail glass.

Blue Star

The unearthly colour produced by mixing blue and orange in this drink is further enhanced by serving it frappé, over crushed ice.

1 measure/1½ tbsp gin
¾ measure/3 tsp Noilly Prat or other dry vermouth
⅓ measure/1½ tsp blue curaçao
1 measure/1½ tbsp orange juice

Shake all the ingredients well with ice, and strain into a cocktail glass full of finely crushed ice. Garnish with a half-slice of orange.

Jockey Club

This 1920s mixture of gin with dashes of this, that and the other came to Europe all the way from a nightclub in the Cuban capital, Havana.

2 measures/3 tbsp gin
⅓ measure/1½ tsp crème de noyau (or amaretto)
dash orange bitters (or orange curaçao)
dash Angostura bitters
⅓ measure/1½ tsp lemon juice

Shake all the ingredients well with ice and strain into a cocktail glass. Garnish with a half-slice of lemon.

RAC

This was created on the eve of the First World War by the barman of the Royal Automobile Club in London's Pall Mall.

1½ measures/6 tsp gin
¾ measure/3 tsp dry vermouth

¾ measure/3 tsp sweet red vermouth
¼ measure/1 tsp orange bitters

Shake well with ice, and strain into a glass. Squeeze a twist of orange rind over the top to release its oil.

Little Red Riding Hood

Vivid summery fruit flavours make a cocktail that tastes as innocent as Grandma, but has a bite more reminiscent of the Wolf!

1 measure/1½ tbsp gin
¾ measure/3 tsp crème de mûre

¾ measure/3 tsp crème de fraise
1½ measures/6 tsp orange juice

Shake the ingredients with ice and strain into a large cocktail glass filled with crushed ice. Garnish with a strawberry, a blackberry and a cherry.

Carla

This fruity concoction owes its character to Dutch genever, which should be used in preference to ordinary London gin.

1½ measures/6 tsp jonge genever
2 measures/3 tbsp orange juice
1 measure/1½ tbsp passion fruit juice
2 measures/3 tbsp lemonade

Shake the first three ingredients together with a couple of handfuls of crushed ice, and pour, unstrained, into a highball glass. Add the lemonade. You could garnish with a slice of orange.

Bartending know-how
In the Netherlands, genever is nearly always drunk neat, accompanied by a chaser of the local beer.

Bridesmaid

This drink sounds as though it would be perfect for a summer wedding, as long as the bridesmaids have fulfilled their duties by the time it's served.

2 measures/3 tbsp gin
1 measure/1½ tbsp lemon juice
¾ measure/3 tsp sugar syrup
dash Angostura bitters
4 measures/6 tbsp sparkling ginger ale

Add the first four ingredients to a tall glass filled with cracked ice, stir well and add the ginger ale. Garnish with a twist of lemon.

Bennett

Dating from the 1920s, this short drink is sometimes seen spelt with only one "t", and with a small quantity of sugar syrup added to it, but this is the original formula, which on the whole I prefer for its sharper edge.

1½ measures/6 tsp gin
½ measure/2 tsp lime juice
2 dashes Angostura bitters

Shake well with ice and strain into a cocktail glass.

César Ritz

Created at the Paris Ritz Hotel, this was named after the legendary chef of the 19th century.

2 measures/3 tbsp gin
⅔ measure/1 tbsp dry vermouth
⅓ measure/1½ tsp cherry brandy
½ measure/2 tsp kirsch

Stir the ingredients gently in a pitcher with ice cubes, until a frost of condensation mists the outside. Strain into a cocktail glass. Add a cocktail cherry that has been liberally dunked in kirsch.

Space

… the final frontier? Not quite, but this is a very moreish modern cocktail recipe made with hazelnut liqueur. A good aperitif.

1½ measures/6 tsp gin
1 measure/1½ tbsp Frangelico (or crème de noisette)
½ measure/2 tsp lemon juice

Shake all the ingredients well with ice, and strain into a rocks glass. Add a couple of pieces of cracked ice.

Bartending know-how
The monk after whom Frangelico is named, and who is credited with its recipe, lived as a hermit in north-west Italy in the 17th century.

Honolulu

This fruity little shooter should be served in a shot glass.

1 measure/1½ tbsp gin
¼ measure/1 tsp pineapple juice
¼ measure/1 tsp orange juice
¼ measure/1 tsp lemon juice

¼ measure/1 tsp pineapple syrup (from a can)
1 drop Angostura bitters

Shake all but the last ingredient with ice and strain into a shot glass. Add a single drop of Angostura to the drink, and knock back in one.

Caruso

Towards the end of his life, the celebrated Italian opera singer Enrico Caruso stayed at the Hotel Sevilla in Cuba, where an obliging barman created this cocktail in his honour.

1 measure/1½ tbsp gin
1 measure/1½ tbsp dry vermouth
1 measure/1½ tbsp green crème de menthe

Shake well with ice and strain into a cocktail glass. Some versions these days use a little less crème de menthe than a whole measure, as the flavour is so strong, but this is the original recipe.

Barbarella

This is a colourful drink named after the title character in the classic sci-fi movie, played by Jane Fonda.

1 measure/1½ tbsp Plymouth gin
1 measure/1½ tbsp dry vermouth
½ measure/2 tsp Galliano
¼ measure/1 tsp blue curaçao
2 measures/3 tbsp sparkling bitter lemon

Shake the first four ingredients well with ice, and strain into a rocks glass that has been half-filled with cracked ice. Add the bitter lemon, and garnish with a slice of lemon.

Damn the Weather

This cocktail has been around since the 1920s, and presumably commemorates a particularly persistent gloomy spell.

1 measure/1½ tbsp gin
½ measure/2 tsp sweet red vermouth
½ measure/2 tsp orange juice
¼ measure/1 tsp orange curaçao

Shake well with ice, and strain into a chilled whisky tumbler. Add a twist of orange wrapped around a cocktail stick.

Park Avenue

This sharp and fruity cocktail takes its name from one of the smartest thoroughfares in New York City.

1½ measures/6 tsp gin
½ measure/2 tsp cherry brandy
½ measure/2 tsp lime juice
¼ measure/1 tsp maraschino

Shake all the ingredients well with ice, and strain into a cocktail glass. Garnish with a cocktail cherry and add a thin slice of lime.

Derby

This classic, old, American short drink is just a barely modified gin. Instead of garnishing the glass with a mint leaf, you could add a couple of mint sprigs to the alcohol in the shaker, and then strain them out.

2 measures/3 tbsp gin
¼ measure/1 tsp peach bitters

Shake with ice and then strain into a liqueur glass. Garnish with a leaf of garden mint.

Red Cloud

Although red clouds at night were once said to be a sailor's delight, you don't have to be ocean-bound to enjoy one of these.

1½ measures/6 tsp gin
¾ measure/3 tsp apricot brandy
½ measure/2 tsp lemon juice
¼ measure/1 tsp grenadine
dash Angostura bitters

Shake all the ingredients well with ice, and strain into a champagne saucer or cocktail glass. Garnish with a half-slice of lemon and a cherry.

Bartending know-how
The oversized label around each Angostura bitters bottle was an administrative error that just stuck!

Maiden's Blush

There were two quite distinct recipes for Maiden's Blush, even in the 1920s. The first mixed gin with orange curaçao, lemon juice and grenadine. This one was a slightly more lethal proposition, and the blush effect in the colour is more apparent, if you need any excuse to up the ante.

2 measures/3 tbsp gin
1 measure/1½ tbsp absinthe
¼ measure/1 tsp grenadine

Shake all the ingredients well with ice, and strain into an ice-cold cocktail glass.

Bartending know-how
Cocktails containing absinthe should be served sparingly. Too many aren't necessarily very nice.

Bee's Knees

The name should give a clue as to the essential ingredient in this rather restorative mixture. The honey and lemon together give the drink a particularly comforting note.

1½ measures/6 tsp gin
¼ measure/1 tsp honey
¼ measure/1 tsp lemon juice

Shake the ingredients very well with ice to integrate the honey, and strain into a cocktail glass.

Cloister

A strong lemony/herbal flavour pervades the Cloister. It is a short drink that delivers a strong kick-start to the tastebuds.

1½ measures/6 tsp gin
½ measure/2 tsp yellow Chartreuse

Grapefruit Cocktail

If you have a grapefruit on the go after making a Cloister, it makes sense to move on to this classic preparation next. Waste not, want not.

1½ measures/6 tsp gin
1 measure/1½ tbsp grapefruit juice
¼ measure/1 tsp maraschino

Shake all the ingredients well with ice, and strain into a champagne saucer or cocktail glass. Garnish with a sliver of grapefruit and a cherry.

½ measure/2 tsp grapefruit juice
¼ measure/1 tsp lemon juice
¼ measure/1 tsp sugar syrup

Shake all the ingredients well with ice, and strain into a cocktail glass. Garnish with a twist of grapefruit rind.

Tangier

A four-city cocktail tour on this page starts in Morocco with this sweetly orangey number. The choice of city for the name distantly reflects the tangerines that go into Mandarine Napoléon.

1 measure/1½ tbsp gin
1 measure/1½ tbsp Cointreau
1 measure/1½ tbsp Mandarine Napoléon

Shake all the ingredients well with ice, and strain into a cocktail glass. Decorate the glass with a spiral twist of orange rind, wrapped around a cocktail stick.

Berliner

A dry, and very grown-up sort of drink, Berliner is full of herbal flavours from the vermouth and kümmel and has a finishing tang of lemon.

1½ measures/6 tsp gin
½ measure/2 tsp dry vermouth
½ measure/2 tsp kümmel
½ measure/2 tsp lemon juice

Shake all the ingredients well with ice, and strain into a chilled cocktail glass. Squeeze a bit of lemon rind over the top, and garnish with a half-slice of lemon.

Parisian

Another 1920s recipe that nicely balances the sweetness of blackcurrant liqueur with the acerbic dryness of good dry French vermouth.

1 measure/1½ tbsp gin
1 measure/1½ tbsp Noilly Prat

Dundee

What else but Scottish ingredients (two of them, in fact) could give a drink a name like this? This is a dry, sour cocktail with quite a kick.

1 measure/1½ tbsp gin
¾ measure/3 tsp Scotch

1 measure/1½ tbsp crème de cassis

Shake all the ingredients well with ice, and strain into a cocktail glass. Add three or four blackcurrants to the glass to add touches of sharpness to the drink. They can be eaten at the end.

½ measure/2 tsp Drambuie
½ measure/2 tsp lemon juice

Shake all the ingredients well with ice, and strain into a whisky tumbler. Squeeze a twist of lemon rind over the drink, and then drop it into the glass.

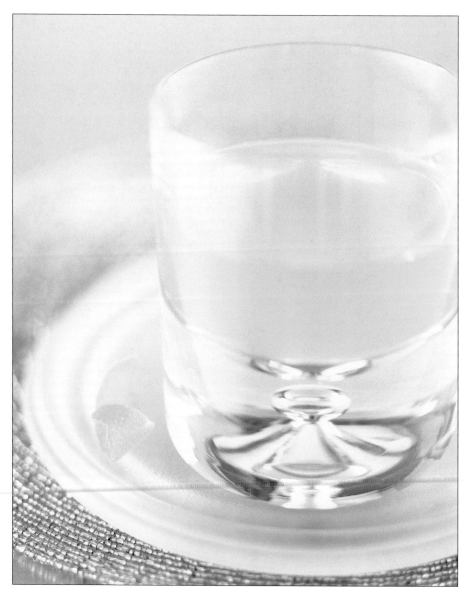

Juan-les-Pins

Once the preferred destination of the Mediterranean jet-set, the Riviera resort is fittingly honoured by this appetizing mixture of gin, an aperitif and a liqueur.

1 measure/1½ tbsp gin
¾ measure/3 tsp white Dubonnet
½ measure/2 tsp apricot brandy
dash lemon juice

Shake all the ingredients well with ice, and strain into a cocktail glass. Garnish with a slice of apricot and a cherry speared by a cocktail stick.

Whiteout

A highly indulgent preparation with which to conclude the gin collection, this is a sweet, chocolate cream cocktail that tastes far more innocuous than it actually is.

1½ measures/6 tsp gin
1 measure/1½ tbsp white crème de cacao
1 measure/1½ tbsp double (heavy) cream

Shake all the ingredients very well with ice to amalgamate the cream fully, and then strain into a chilled cocktail glass. Grate a small piece of white chocolate over the surface.

Bloodhound

The drink takes its name from the rather gory colour and texture produced by including whole strawberries in the blend.

1½ measures/6 tsp gin
½ measure/2 tsp dry vermouth
½ measure/2 tsp sweet red vermouth
¼ measure/1 tsp crème de fraise
6 strawberries

Put all the ingredients into a liquidizer with ice, and blend for about 20 seconds. Strain into a cocktail glass, and garnish with a final whole strawberry dipped in crème de fraise.

Princeton

This cocktail was created in the early 20th century to honour one of America's Ivy League universities. It was originally made with a sweet gin called Old Tom, but the drier version tastes better.

1½ measures/6 tsp gin
¾ measure/3 tsp ruby port
¼ measure/1 tsp orange bitters

Stir the ingredients together with plenty of ice in a large pitcher, and then strain into a rocks glass or cocktail glass. Squeeze a piece of lemon rind over the surface to release a spray of oil, and then drop it into the drink.

Bartending know-how
It is estimated that, at the time the Gin Act was introduced in 1736, average consumption in London had hit something like two-thirds of a bottle per head *per day*.

Vodka

Vodka may not seem the most obviously useful ingredient in the cocktail cupboard, in the sense that it is typically just a neutral, colourless spirit that at most can only add a further shot of alcohol to a mixed drink. However, many of the modern cocktails are based on the principle of blending a range of different, often exotic fruit flavours over an alcohol base that doesn't interfere with the taste of them. If there are surprisingly few vodka cocktails from the classic era, that is because vodka wasn't then generally commercially available. Some of the recipes here use one of today's ultra-fashionable flavoured vodkas.

Screwdriver

The Screwdriver is the original vodka and orange, so named – as the story has it – after an American oil-rig worker developed the habit of stirring his drink with a screwdriver. Presumably, swizzle-sticks are in rather short supply on oil-rigs. As a member of the classic cocktail repertoire, it probably only dates from the 1950s, which is when vodka made its first, tentative appearance on Western markets. The rest is history.

2 measures/3 tbsp vodka
4 measures/6 tbsp orange juice

Add the ingredients, spirit first, to a rocks glass or whisky tumbler loaded with ice cubes, and throw in a slice of orange. Made with freshly squeezed rather than commercial juice, the drink tastes more grown-up and appears to pack more of a punch, as the juice is naturally thinner than concentrate orange juice from a carton.

Moscow Mule

One of the classic American vodka-based cocktails, the Moscow Mule was invented at a Los Angeles restaurant in 1947 as part of the first US sales drive for the Smirnoff brand. It should contain enough vodka to give the drink a real kick, as befits a mule.

2 measures/3 tbsp vodka
¼ measure/1 tsp lime juice
3 measures/4½ tbsp sparkling ginger ale

Pour the vodka and lime juice into a highball glass half-filled with ice. Mix together well with a bar spoon. Top up the mixture with ginger ale, and add a few halved slices of lime to the cocktail.

Black Russian

The true Black Russian is simply equal measures of vodka and Tia Maria, or Kahlúa, mixed with ice cubes in a tumbler. However, the fashion in recent years has been to serve it as a long drink in a big glass, topped up with cola.

Proportions of the classic Black Russian vary according to taste. Two parts vodka to one part Tia Maria on ice, with no mixer, makes a very adult drink. Certain aficionados insist on Kahlúa rather than Tia Maria with the vodka. Either way, it is as well not to adulterate the drink with cola.

White Russian

The White Russian is a creamy version of the Black, which needs shaking rather than stirring, so as to incorporate the cream.

1 measure/1½ tbsp vodka
1 measure/1½ tbsp Kahlúa or Tia Maria
1 measure/1½ tbsp whipping cream

Shake all the ingredients well with ice, and strain into a cocktail glass.

Blenheim

A further twist on the basic Black Russian idea, Blenheim uses orange juice instead of cola, if you want a non-alcoholic mixer in there. The resulting colour is not the loveliest, but the flavour is better than it sounds.

1½ measures/6 tsp vodka
¾ measure/3 tsp Tia Maria
¾ measure/3 tsp orange juice

Shake all the ingredients well with ice, and strain into a cocktail glass.

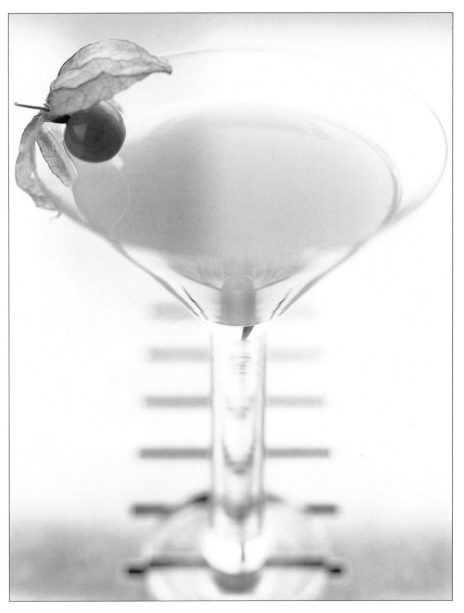

Golden Russian

This is a quite distinct drink from the preceding two Russians, in which the vodka acts to take a little of the sweetness off the liqueur, while the lime sharpens it all up still further. It's a very ingenious (and powerful) mixture, and one that should not be taken lightly.

1½ measures/6 tsp vodka
1 measure/1½ tbsp Galliano
¼ measure/1 tsp lime juice

Pour all the ingredients into a rocks glass over plenty of cracked ice, and stir. Add a slice of lime.

Bullshot

The Bullshot is a sort of Bloody Mary, only with beef consommé replacing the tomato juice. It too is thought to have amazing restorative powers as a reviving breakfast drink after the previous night's indulgence. It can be handy if you really can't bear to eat anything, but drink some water first.

2 measures/3 tbsp vodka
4 measures/6 tbsp cold beef consommé
   (classically Campbell's)
½ measure/2 tsp lemon juice
¼ measure/1 tsp Worcestershire sauce
2 dashes Tabasco
pinch celery salt
pinch cayenne pepper

Mix all the ingredients with ice in a pitcher, and then strain into a highball glass half-filled with ice.

Bloody Mary

Everybody has his or her own recipe for the next best hangover cure after aspirin. Some strange people even put tomato ketchup into it. Others round out the alcohol with a splash of dry sherry. Here is my own formula.

Put a slice of lemon and 2–3 ice cubes in a tall glass, add 5ml/1 tsp Worcestershire sauce, 5ml/1 tsp freshly squeezed lemon juice, a pinch of celery salt, about six drops of Tabasco and six twists of the black pepper mill. Stir to coat the ice. Fill the glass to about 4cm/1½in from the top with tomato juice and pour in a generous measure of vodka. Stir well.

Dickson's Bloody Mary

This recipe has plenty of spicy character, with horseradish, sherry and Tabasco. Made with chilli or pepper vodka, it is a much hotter proposition than the standard recipe.

Gipsy

The ingredients in this recipe make for an exotically scented, and slightly bittersweet mixture. It would make a highly unusual digestif for the end of a grand dinner.

2 measures/3 tbsp vodka
1 measure/1½ tbsp Bénédictine
dash Angostura bitters

Add the ingredients to a whisky tumbler or Old-Fashioned glass half-full of cracked ice, and stir gently.

2 measures/3 tbsp chilli-flavoured
   vodka
1 measure/1½ tbsp fino sherry
7 measures/150ml/¼ pint tomato juice
1 measure/1½ tbsp lemon juice
2–3 dashes Tabasco
10–15ml/2–3 tsp Worcestershire sauce
2.5ml/½ tsp creamed horseradish
5ml/1 tsp celery salt
salt and ground black pepper
celery stalk, stuffed green olives and a
   cherry tomato, to decorate

Fill a pitcher with cracked ice and add the vodka, sherry and tomato juice. Stir well. Add the lemon juice, Tabasco, Worcestershire sauce and horseradish. Stir again. Add the celery salt, salt and pepper, and stir until the pitcher has frosted and the contents are chilled. Strain into a tall tumbler, half-filled with ice cubes. Add a stick of celery.

Mint Collins

The original Tom Collins recipe has been adapted since the 1950s to be made with vodka rather than gin. This refreshing, summery variation also adds the cool flavour of mint for extra class.

2 measures/3 tbsp vodka
⅓ measure/1½ tsp green crème de menthe
1 measure/1½ tbsp lemon juice
dash sugar syrup
5 measures/120ml/4fl oz soda water

Half-fill a highball glass with cracked ice, and then add the first four ingredients. Give the drink a good stir and then top up with the soda. Float a sprig of fresh mint on the top.

Chilli Vodkatini

Not quite a Vodkatini, but almost. This recipe produces a hot, savoury drink that is stirred in the manner of the original Dry Martini, and served with a couple of chilli peppers in it.

1 measure/1½ tbsp chilli or pepper vodka
¼ measure/1 tsp dry French vermouth
2 small pickled or vodka-soaked chillies and
   1 pitted green olive, to garnish

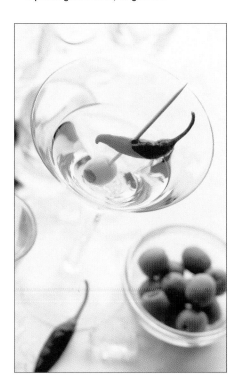

Vodkatini

This variation on a Dry Martini was popularized by James Bond. Famously, it should be "shaken, not stirred", which gives the drink a cloudiness not achieved in the classic recipe.

The mixture is basically that of a classic Dry Martini, but with vodka replacing the gin. Since vodka lacks the aromatic character of gin, it is generally served with a twist of lemon rind immersed in the drink, as well as being squeezed over it.

Add the chilli or pepper vodka to a bar glass of ice and mix for about 30 seconds, until the outside of the glass is frosted over. Add the vermouth to a chilled cocktail glass, swirl it around to wet the inside of the glass, and then pour it away. Cut one of the pickled chillies in half and discard the seeds. Thread it through the pitted green olive, and then thread the stuffed olive on to a cocktail stick with the other chilli. Strain the cocktail into the prepared glass. Add the olive and chilli decoration to the drink before serving.

Bartending know-how
There are two kinds of pepper vodka. Some is flavoured with red chillies, but most is spiced with crushed black peppercorns.

Après-Ski

Certainly not to be tried before skiing anyway. The intriguing mixture of aniseed, mint and lemon in this drink is quite a challenge. Somehow the mint emphasizes the flavour of the Pernod. One should be enough, not least because the drink has an exceedingly long aftertaste.

1 measure/1½ tbsp vodka
1 measure/1½ tbsp Pernod
½ measure/2 tsp green crème de menthe
5 measures/120ml/4fl oz sparkling lemonade

Shake the first three ingredients with ice, and then strain into a highball glass with a couple of ice cubes in it. Add the lemonade. Garnish the drink with a sprig of mint and a slice of lemon.

Harvey Wallbanger

This is the next step up from a Screwdriver, with a dash of Galliano added. It is a 1970s recipe that supposedly derives its name from having left a gentleman called Harvey, who had downed several of them, in the walking-into-walls state. There is no need to go quite that far, but it's easy to see why the formula became such a popular one in nightclubs.

2 measures/3 tbsp vodka
¾ measure/3 tsp Galliano
5 measures/120ml/4fl oz orange juice

Add the vodka and orange juice to a highball glass half-filled with cracked ice. Pour the Galliano carefully over the top so that it floats above the other ingredients. Garnish with a half-slice of orange, decorated with a canelle knife.

Kiss and Tell

A thoroughly exotic mixture of flavours goes into this modern cocktail, and the resulting throbbingly vibrant colour is something to be seen.

1 measure/1½ tbsp vodka
½ measure/2 tsp Galliano
¼ measure/1 tsp dry vermouth
¼ measure/1 tsp blue curaçao
2 measures/3 tbsp orange juice
1 measure/1½ tbsp passion fruit juice

Bartending know-how
The blue Bols curaçao is so popular that it is probably now the flagship product of their liqueur range.

Shake all the ingredients with roughly crushed ice and pour everything out into a tall glass. Garnish with a half-slice of orange and a cherry.

Liberator

Here is another of those cocktails full of blended, tropical fruit flavours, to which a vodka base lends itself so well.

1½ measures/6 tsp vodka
½ measure/2 tsp Midori or other melon liqueur
2 measures/3 tbsp mango juice
½ measure/2 tsp lime juice

Shake all the ingredients well with ice, and strain into a cocktail glass. Garnish with a neatly cut sliver of mango and a slice of lime.

Barbara

This is a variation on the White Russian, but with a chocolatey flavour replacing the original coffee.

1 measure/1½ tbsp vodka
1 measure/1½ tbsp white crème de cacao
½ measure/2 tsp double (heavy) cream

Shake all the ingredients well with ice, and strain into a cocktail glass. The surface of the drink can be sprinkled with grated chocolate.

Piranha

This is one of those deceptive cocktails that tastes relatively harmless, but in fact packs quite a bite, much like the predatory flesh-eating fish after which it is named.

1½ measures/6 tsp vodka
1 measure/1½ tbsp of brown crème de cacao
1 measure/1½ tbsp ice-cold cola

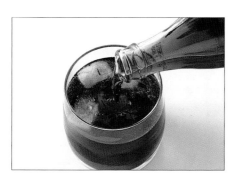

Pour the alcohol into a rocks glass containing plenty of cracked ice and stir vigorously, before adding the cola.

Bartending know-how
Brands of cola have proliferated like wildfire ever since the success of the original Coca-Cola. There are low-sugar and caffeine-free versions, and there is now a French brand aimed at the Muslim market.

Camshaft

I am not at all certain how this drink came to be named after part of a car engine. Perhaps the fruit juices in it act as sliding parts to facilitate the passage of the alcohol.

1 measure/1½ tbsp vodka
½ measure/2 tsp Campari
1 measure/1½ tbsp passion fruit juice
1 measure/1½ tbsp orange juice
1 measure/1½ tbsp sparkling lemonade

Pour the ingredients in this order into a rocks glass half-full of cracked ice. Stir briefly and gently, being careful not to neutralize the fizz in the lemonade. Garnish with a half-slice of orange and a half-slice of lemon.

Katinka

This fruity mixture achieves a nice balance of sweet and sour flavours, and is revved up with the added horsepower of the vodka. A good Russian brand such as Stolichnaya would be the optimum choice for the drink.

SOS

Lemon vodka is called for in this drink. Russian types are termed limonnaya and flavoured with natural lemon essence, or there is a mixed citrus version made by the Swedish Absolut company called Citron.

1 measure/1½ tbsp lemon vodka
1 measure/1½ tbsp peach schnapps
2 measures/3 tbsp unsweetened mandarin
   juice (from a can, if necessary)
¼ measure/1 tsp grenadine

Shake all the ingredients well with ice, and strain into a large cocktail glass. Garnish with a slice of lemon and a mandarin segment on a cocktail stick, and add a short straw.

1½ measures/6 tsp vodka
1 measure/1½ tbsp apricot brandy
½ measure/2 tsp lime juice

Shake all the ingredients well with ice, and strain into a cocktail glass heaped with slivered ice. Add a slice of lime.

Slow Comfortable Screw

The 1970s idea of a joke in the drink's name may be a touch embarrassing now, but the mixture is a good one, and the drink was something of a modern classic a generation ago.

1 measure/1½ tbsp vodka
¾ measure/3 tsp Southern Comfort
¾ measure/3 tsp sloe gin
5 measures/120ml/4fl oz orange juice

Cosmopolitan

This drink has a similar bracing flavour to a Sea Breeze, but the sweet liqueur shows through the bitter juices.

1½ measures/6 tsp vodka
1 measure/1½ tbsp Cointreau
1 measure/1½ tbsp cranberry juice
½ measure/2 tsp lime juice

Shake all the ingredients well with ice, and strain into a large cocktail glass. Dangle a twist of orange in the drink.

Add the first three ingredients to a highball glass half-packed with ice. Stir to combine, and then top up with the orange juice. Garnish with a cocktail cherry on a stick for the essential seventies touch, and add two long straws. A plastic novelty will add that final note of sheer class, as will throwing back three of them and then slow-dancing with somebody ghastly.

Bailey's Comet

The spirit turns the popular creamy liqueur into a rather stiffer proposition.

1 measure/1½ tbsp vodka
1 measure/1½ tbsp Bailey's

Combine the ingredients with cracked ice in a rocks glass. The quantity can safely be doubled to save time, as you're bound to want another.

Sea Breeze

One of today's most requested cocktails, Sea Breeze was one of the first popular cocktails to use cranberry juice. Ocean Spray is one of the most famous brands, but the supermarkets nearly all have a proprietary version.

2 measures/3 tbsp vodka
2 measures/3 tbsp grapefruit juice
3 measures/4½ tbsp cranberry juice

Shake all the ingredients well with plenty of ice, and pour everything into a chilled highball glass. Add a wedge of lime and a few cranberries.

Bartending know-how
Cranberry juice is a sugar-and-water product. It is possible to buy apple juice with cranberry if you want neither sugar nor water.

Pompanski

This drink specifically calls for one of the premium Polish vodkas. Its soft texture and rounded feel in the mouth are a world away from neutral commercial vodka.

1 measure/1½ tbsp Wodka Wyborowa
½ measure/2 tsp dry vermouth
¼ measure/1 tsp Cointreau
1 measure/1½ tbsp grapefruit juice

Shake all the ingredients together with three or four ice cubes and then pour everything, unstrained, into a rocks glass. Add a twist of grapefruit rind.

Hammer Horror

Use the best vanilla ice cream you can find for this, and preferably one that is made with whole egg and real vanilla, for extra richness.

1 measure/1½ tbsp vodka
1 measure/1½ tbsp Kahlúa
60ml/4 tbsp vanilla ice cream

Add all the ingredients to a liquidizer with cracked ice, blend for a few seconds and then strain into a cocktail glass. Sprinkle the surface of the drink with grated dark chocolate.

French Horn

The drink is so called because it calls for a particular variety of French liqueur called Chambord, made from black raspberries. If you can't find it, substitute ordinary crème de framboise. Its sweetness is thrown into relief with the neutrality of the vodka and the sharpness of the lemon juice.

1 measure/1½ tbsp vodka
¾ measure/3 tsp Chambord (or crème de framboise)
½ measure/2 tsp lemon juice

Stir the ingredients in a pitcher with plenty of ice. Strain into a cocktail glass and garnish with a whole raspberry.

Hot Cherry

Solve the Russo-Polish dispute as to which of them originally invented vodka by combining both nationalities (in even-handed measure of course) in this exciting cocktail. The tonic water adds a pleasantly bitter note to the rich cherry fruitiness of the mixture.

1 measure/1½ tbsp Stolichnaya vodka
1 measure/1½ tbsp Wisniowka (Polish cherry vodka)
2 measures/3 tbsp tonic water

Shake the vodkas with plenty of cracked ice, strain into a rocks glass containing two ice cubes and add the tonic. Garnish with a cherry.

Kir Lethale

The raisins for this cocktail should be soaked overnight in vodka to give the drink that extra kick. This is a party recipe to serve six.

6 vodka-soaked raisins
30ml/2 tbsp vodka
3 measures/4½ tbsp crème de cassis
1 bottle brut champagne or dry sparkling wine, chilled

Place a vodka-soaked raisin at the bottom of each glass. Add ¼ measure/ 1 tsp plain vodka or the vodka from the steeped raisins, if using, to each glass. Add ½ measure/2 tsp crème de cassis to each and finish the drinks with the champagne or sparkling wine.

Pushkin's Punch

This powerful cocktail is named after the great Russian writer. Use a good sparkling wine from Australia or California.

1 measure/1½ tbsp vodka
1 measure/1½ tbsp Grand Marnier
dash lime juice
dash orange bitters (or orange curaçao)
dry sparkling wine

Shake the first four ingredients with ice, and strain into a chilled, large wine goblet. Top up with sparkling wine.

Soft Fruit and Ginger Cup

This colourful medley of soft fruits is steeped in vodka and served with an icy blend of sorbet and ginger ale. You will definitely need to use spoons. The recipe serves four, and can be used as a summer dinner-party dessert.

115g/4oz strawberries, hulled
115g/4oz raspberries, hulled
50g/2oz blueberries
15ml/1 tbsp caster (superfine) sugar
4 measures/6 tbsp vodka
600ml/1 pint still ginger ale
4 large scoops orange sorbet
1 measure/1½ tbsp grenadine

Cut the strawberries in half and put them in a bowl with the raspberries, blueberries and sugar. Pour over the vodka and toss lightly. Cover and chill for at least 30 minutes. Put the ginger ale and sorbet in a blender or food processor and process until smooth. Pour into four bowl-shaped glasses and

add a couple of ice cubes to each glass of sorbet mixture. Spoon ¼ measure/ 1 tsp grenadine over the ice cubes in each glass, then spoon the vodka-steeped fruits on top of the sorbet mixture and ice cubes. Garnish each glass with a physalis and serve.

Vodka and Kumquat Lemonade

This is a mild-sounding name for what is a strong concoction of kumquat and peppercorn-flavoured vodka and white curaçao. The recipe comfortably serves two, in long glasses.

90g/3oz kumquats
5 measures/120ml/4fl oz vodka
3 black peppercorns
⅔ measure/1 tbsp white curaçao
⅔ measure/1 tbsp lemon juice
7 measures/150ml/¼ pint sparkling mineral or soda water
fresh mint leaves

Thickly slice the kumquats and add to the vodka in an airtight jar with the cracked black peppercorns. Set aside for at least a couple of hours or overnight if possible. Fill a pitcher with cracked ice and then add the curaçao, the lemon juice and the kumquat-flavoured vodka with the sliced kumquats (but not the peppercorns). Using a long swizzle-stick, stir together well. Add the mineral or soda water and a few fresh mint leaves and gently stir everything together. Pour the drink into chilled glasses of ice. Add slices of kumquats to the glasses and garnish with extra mint sprigs.

Woo Woo

A creation of the 1980s, Woo Woo was one of the first cocktail recipes to use peach schnapps. Archer's Peach County was the brand preferred, and the recipe is still a popular one on today's cocktail lists.

1 measure/1½ tbsp vodka
1½ measures/6 tsp peach schnapps
4 measures/6 tbsp cranberry juice

Shake all the ingredients well with ice, and strain into a highball glass half-filled with cracked ice.

Bartending know-how
Peach schnapps is not really a true schnapps, but a sort of schnapps-based liqueur. Archer's now make lime and cranberry versions to supplement the original peach.

Nevsky Prospekt

The Russian reference here is to a boulevard in Moscow. You can add ¼ measure/1 tsp sugar syrup if you feel it needs a touch of extra sweetness, but I prefer it quite sour.

1½ measures/6 tsp Stolichnaya vodka
½ measure/2 tsp light rum
½ measure/2 tsp orange curaçao
¼ measure/1 tsp lime juice

Shake all the ingredients well with ice, and strain into a cocktail glass. Garnish with a half-slice of lime.

Green Dragon

You will find one glass of this dry, savoury and extremely strong cocktail is more than enough. Sip it slowly, or be brave and take it at a couple of gulps. Then lie down.

Blackhawk

A lustrous purple is more the colour here than black, and the combination of fruit flavours is quite enchanting. This is a very moreish short drink with an appealing balance of sweet and sour.

1½ measures/6 tsp vodka
½ measure/2 tsp crème de mûre
½ measure/2 tsp lime juice

Shake all the ingredients well with ice, and strain into a cocktail glass. Add a whole, perfectly ripe blackberry and a half-slice of lime.

2 measures/3 tbsp Stolichnaya vodka
1 measure/1½ tbsp green Chartreuse

Shake the ingredients well with ice, and strain into a cocktail glass.

Blue Shark

Blue curaçao mixes so well with clear spirits that it would seem a shame not to include a vodka-based recipe, and here is a popular American one.

1 measure/1½ tbsp vodka
1 measure/1½ tbsp tequila
½ measure/2 tsp blue curaçao

Shake all the ingredients well with ice, and strain into a small rocks glass. Squeeze a little orange rind over the drink to release the oil, but don't add the rind itself.

Bartending know-how

The kümmel you will buy for making a Boyar will most probably be the pre-eminent Wolfschmidt brand. It has been sold in the UK since the late Victorian era, having originally made its name in the Baltic state of Latvia.

Genoa

This is something like a strong Screwdriver with the bittering element of Campari adding savoury appeal.

1½ measures/6 tsp vodka
2 measures/3 tbsp orange juice
¾ measure/3 tsp Campari

Shake all the ingredients well with ice, and strain into a rocks glass containing a couple of cubes of ice. Add a twist of orange rind.

Boyar

This very dry and herb-tinged mixture would make a good appetite-whetter at a party where nibbles are going to be served. The tiny quantity of kümmel shines through, and leaves a very appetizing aftertaste in its wake.

Borodino

Let's get serious. This is a strong cocktail, with the ingredients in the 37.5% to 40% alcohol range, but the result is a virginal-looking white drink.

1 measure/1½ tbsp vodka
1 measure/1½ tbsp gin
1 measure/1½ tbsp Cointreau

Shake all the ingredients well with ice, and strain into a cocktail glass. Add a small piece of orange rind.

2 measures/3 tbsp vodka
½ measure/2 tsp dry vermouth
¼ measure/1 tsp kümmel

Shake with ice, and strain into a cocktail glass. The drink doesn't need a garnish.

Sex on the Beach

A variation on Woo Woo, this version has more fruit juice. The name has, not surprisingly, kept it popular in seaside resorts, as the next best resort after sex.

1 measure/1½ tbsp vodka
1 measure/1½ tbsp peach schnapps

3 measures/4½ tbsp cranberry juice
3 measures/4½ tbsp pineapple juice

Half-fill a highball glass with cracked ice, add all the ingredients in the above order, and stir vigorously. Garnish with pieces of pineapple and orange.

Soviet Cocktail

This is an American drink intended as a sort of grudging acknowledgement of its old adversary, the USSR.

1½ measures/6 tsp vodka
½ measure/2 tsp dry vermouuth
½ measure/2 tsp medium-dry (amontillado) sherry

Shake all the ingredients well with ice, and strain into a cocktail glass. Squeeze a twist of lemon rind over the top and drop it into the drink.

Prussian Salute

This is one of those hardcore cocktails that's all alcohol with no mixers. The sweet fruit notes in it help to soften its impact a little – but not much.

1½ measures/6 tsp vodka
½ measure/2 tsp crème de mûre
½ measure/2 tsp slivovitz
½ measure/2 tsp Cointreau

Shake all the ingredients well with ice, and strain into a cocktail glass. Garnish with a slice of lemon.

Kempinsky Fizz

A luxuriously fruity, fizzy mixture with a delicate pinkish colour, this would kick off a dinner party in fine style.

1½ measures/6 tsp vodka
½ measure/2 tsp crème de cassis
¼ measure/1 tsp lemon juice
4 measures/6 tbsp sparkling ginger ale

Half-fill a chilled tall glass with ice, add the first three ingredients, stir briskly and then top up with ginger ale.

Bartending know-how
The original home of syrupy crème de cassis is Burgundy in eastern France, where much is made in Dijon. As a classic fruit liqueur, it dates back to the mid-19th century, and its principal export market today – somewhat surprisingly – is Japan, where they mix it with soda.

Rum

Before the advent of vodka cocktails, rum was the spirit with which all the exotic flavours were mixed. Coming from the tropical climates of the Caribbean and South America, it was felt to lend itself to all kinds of racy preparations, so unlike the comparative staidness of gin, whisky and brandy. There are basically three grades in the cocktail repertoire: white, light (or golden) and dark. The top-strength naval rums, known as "overproof", are sometimes added in droplets to a mixture: not just to fortify it, but to concentrate the flavour of what is still an under-appreciated spirit.

Tom and Jerry

A cold weather drink invented in the 1850s by the legendary Jerry Thomas of St Louis, Missouri, Tom and Jerry is one of the oldest cocktails in this book. It is said that Mr Thomas would serve these at the first snows of winter. This recipe serves four to six people.

For the batter:
3 eggs
45ml/3 tbsp caster (superfine) sugar
pinch bicarbonate of soda (baking soda)
1 measure/1½ tbsp dark rum
1.5ml/¼ tsp ground cinnamon
pinch ground cloves
pinch allspice

Separate the eggs and beat the whites into stiff peaks, adding 15ml/1 tbsp of the sugar with the bicarbonate. Mix the yolks separately with the rum, the rest of the sugar and the spices. Then fold in the whites with a metal spoon.

For each drink:
1 measure/1½ tbsp dark rum
1 measure/1½ tbsp brandy
4 measures/6 tbsp boiling milk

Using heatproof glasses, put in 15ml/1 tbsp of the batter and 1 measure/1½ tbsp each of rum and brandy, then top up with boiled milk. Dust with nutmeg.

Bacardi Cocktail

The original recipe, this must (legally, in the USA) be made with the world's biggest-selling white rum brand. It's short and sour and altogether perfect.

1½ measures/6 tsp Bacardi white rum
juice of half a lime
¼ measure/1 tsp grenadine

Shake all the ingredients well with ice, and strain into a cocktail glass. Add a slice of lime. (Add a measure of gin to turn it into a Bacardi Special, a variation created in the 1920s.)

Caribbean Breeze

This bang-up-to-date mixture of exotic fruit flavours will have party guests coming back for more.

1½ measures/6 tsp dark rum
½ measure/2 tsp crème de banane
3 measures/4½ tbsp pineapple juice
2 measures/3 tbsp cranberry juice
¼ measure/1 tsp lime cordial

Shake all the ingredients well with ice, and strain into a large wine goblet, generously filled with crushed ice. Garnish with a slice of pineapple and a wedge of lime.

Cuba Libre

This is a brand-specific cocktail if ever there was one. Created in Cuba – where Bacardi was then produced – in the late 19th century, the novelty value of Cuba Libre lay in its use of Coca-Cola, a newfangled tonic beverage, then less than ten years on the market.

juice and rind of half a lime
2 measures/3 tbsp Bacardi white rum
5 measures/120ml/4 fl oz Coca-Cola

Squeeze the juice directly into a highball glass half-filled with cracked ice, and then put the empty rind in too. Add the rum, stir, and finally top up with ice-cold Coca-Cola.

Ti Punch

This is a great favourite in the originally French Caribbean islands.

1 lime
2 measures/3 tbsp French Caribbean white rum
¼ measure/1 tsp sugar syrup

Cut the lime into wedges and put them in a wide-based rocks glass. Pound and crush them with a blunt instrument to release the juices, but leave all the residue in the glass. Add the syrup and the rum, and plenty of cracked ice.

Saoco

I have drunk this cocktail on Barbados served in half a hollowed-out coconut shell, but it does nearly as well served in a plain glass tumbler. Coconut milk is the watery liquid that is released from the centre of a coconut when the end is pierced, and not to be confused with canned coconut cream.

2 measures/3 tbsp white rum
4 measures/6 tbsp coconut milk

Shake both the ingredients well with ice, and then strain into a rocks glass that has been half-filled with finely crushed ice. Drink through two short straws.

Waikiki Beach

This creamy, nutty, exotic cocktail has the power to call up memories of Caribbean beach holidays gone by.

1½ measures/6 tsp white rum
½ measure/2 tsp amaretto
½ measure/2 tsp canned coconut cream
2 measures/3 tbsp pineapple juice
1 measure/1½ tbsp passion fruit juice
1 measure/1½ tbsp double (heavy) cream

Shake all the ingredients well with ice, and strain into a bowl-shaped cocktail glass half-filled with cracked ice. Garnish with a cube of pineapple and a cocktail cherry.

Mary Pickford

A 1920s recipe in tribute to one of the greats among the first generation of silent movie stars.

1½ measures/6 tsp white rum
1½ measures/6 tsp pineapple juice
¼ measure/1 tsp grenadine
dash maraschino

Shake all the ingredients well with ice, and strain into a cocktail glass filled with crushed ice. Garnish with a cocktail cherry.

Daiquiri

The Daiquiri is one of the most adapted and abused cocktails in the repertoire. Created in the 1890s, it is named after a town in Cuba and was originally nothing more than a white rum sour. Despite its extreme simplicity, this really is one of the all-time perfect cocktail recipes, standing proud above the fashionable fruit versions mentioned below.

2 measures/3 tbsp white rum
juice of half a lime or a quarter of a lemon
5ml/1 tsp caster (superfine) sugar

Fruit Daiquiri

The original Daiquiri recipe of white rum shaken with lemon or lime juice and a pinch of sugar can be adapted by adding a measure of any of the fruit liqueurs to it, with about 50g/2oz of the

Shake all the ingredients well with ice to dissolve the sugar, and strain into a well-chilled cocktail glass. Serve ungarnished.

equivalent puréed fruit as well. The sugar can then be left out. A strawberry version, made with crème de fraise and pulped fruit, is especially enticing, and banana is a crowd-pleaser too.

Presidente

Another 1920s Cuban recipe, this is named in honour of one of the island's old military rulers.

2 measures/3 tbsp white rum
1 measure/1½ tbsp orange curaçao
½ measure/2 tsp dry vermouth
¼ measure/1 tsp grenadine

Stir the ingredients with ice in a pitcher to chill them well, and then strain into a frozen rocks glass. Add a slice of lemon, decorated around the edges with a canelle knife.

Planter's Punch

This long, refreshing, old colonial drink originates from the sugar plantations that are dotted throughout the West Indian islands.

1 measure/1½ tbsp fresh lime juice
1 measure/1½ tbsp orange juice
2 measures/3 tbsp dark rum
½ measure/2 tsp grenadine
dash Angostura bitters
soda water or lemonade, chilled

Columbus

A simple and appealing mixture of sweet and sour, Columbus must absolutely be made with light rum, but if that's the only colour you haven't got, use a half-and-half mixture of dark and white.

1½ measures/6 tsp light rum
¾ measure/3 tsp apricot brandy
1 measure/1½ tbsp lime juice

Shake all the ingredients well with ice, and strain into a cocktail glass. Garnish with a slice of lime.

Squeeze the lime and orange juices and add them to a pitcher of ice. Add the dark rum and the grenadine, and mix them together well for about 20 seconds. Add a dash of Angostura bitters to the bottom of a wide tumbler filled with cracked ice cubes. Strain the rum and grenadine mixture into the chilled tumbler. Finish with plenty of chilled soda water or lemonade, according to taste.

Garnish with two skewered peach slices and a physalis, complete with its leaves attached.

Mai Tai

This is a very refreshing, long but strong party drink that slides down easily – just before you do!

1 measure/1½ tbsp light rum
1 measure/1½ tbsp dark rum
1 measure/1½ tbsp apricot brandy
3 measures/4½ tbsp orange juice
3 measures/4½ tbsp pineapple juice
1 measure/1½ tbsp grenadine

Shake the first five ingredients well with ice, and strain into a highball glass half-filled with cracked ice. Slowly pour the grenadine into the glass, letting it sink to the bottom of the drink to make a glowing red layer. The cocktail could be lavishly garnished with tropical fruits.

Monkey Wrench

Deliciously refreshing, despite its indelicate name, this makes a fine drink for a summer afternoon in the garden.

1½ measures/6 tsp white rum
3 measures/4½ tbsp grapefruit juice
3 measures/4½ tbsp sparkling lemonade

Half-fill a highball glass with roughly cracked ice, and add the rum and grapefruit juice. Stir briskly, before topping up with the sparkling lemonade. Decorate with intertwined twists of grapefruit and lemon rind in a suitably artistic arrangement.

Blue Hawaiian

This drink can be decorated as flamboyantly as Carmen Miranda's headdress with a mixture of fruits and leaves. It is an eye-catching, colourful cocktail that you'll find very drinkable.

1 measure/1½ tbsp blue curaçao
1 measure/1½ tbsp coconut cream
2 measures/3 tbsp light rum
2 measures/3 tbsp pineapple juice
leaves and wedge of pineapple, slice of prickly pear or orange, a wedge of lime and a maraschino cherry, to garnish

Escape Route

Punt e Mes, made by the Carpano company of Turin, is one of the classic vermouth brands, and is a must for this elegant cocktail.

1 measure/1½ tbsp light rum
1 measure/1½ tbsp Punt e Mes
½ measure/2 tsp crème de fraise
4 measures/6 tbsp sparkling lemonade

Half-fill a highball glass with cracked ice, and add the first three ingredients. Stir vigorously before topping up with the lemonade. Garnish with a slice of lemon and a couple of mint leaves.

Put the curaçao, coconut cream and light rum in a blender with a few cubes of ice. Process very briefly until the colour is even. Add the pineapple juice to the blender and process the mixture once more until frothy. Spoon crushed ice into a large cocktail glass or goblet until three-quarters full. Strain the cocktail from the blender over the crushed ice.

Garnish with a wedge of pineapple, a slice of prickly pear or orange, a wedge of lime and a maraschino cherry.

Zombie

This legendary 1930s recipe was created at Don the Beachcomber restaurant in Hollywood, reportedly as a hangover cure! It has everything but the kitchen sink in it, and yet is a harmonious (and dynamic) mixture.

1 measure/1½ tbsp light rum
½ measure/2 tsp dark rum
½ measure/2 tsp white rum
1 measure/1½ tbsp orange curaçao
¼ measure/1 tsp Pernod
1 measure/1½ tbsp lemon juice
1 measure/1½ tbsp orange juice
1 measure/1½ tbsp pineapple juice
½ measure/2 tsp papaya juice
¼ measure/1 tsp grenadine
½ measure/2 tsp orgeat (almond syrup)
¼ measure/1 tsp overproof rum

Blend all but the last ingredient with ice, and strain into an ice-packed highball glass. Sprinkle with overproof rum. Garnish with a slice of pineapple, a slice of lime and a mint sprig.

Piña Colada

This has to be one of the most popular cocktails worldwide, with a name meaning "strained pineapple". For that extra Caribbean touch, the drink may be served in a hollowed-out pineapple shell, which also means that you can liquidize the flesh for the juice in the recipe, but a bowl-shaped cocktail glass is the next best thing.

2 measures/3 tbsp white rum
2 measures/3 tbsp pineapple juice
1½ measures/6 tsp coconut cream
5ml/1 tsp caster (superfine) sugar (if freshly blended fruit is used)

Shake all the ingredients well with ice, and strain into a cocktail goblet. Garnish with a slice of pineapple and a cherry. (If you can't get hold of coconut cream, the equivalent quantity of any coconut liqueur such as Malibu may be used to good effect.)

Passion Punch

Although it is not really a punch at all, the combination of passion fruit and grape juices in this recipe is a winning one. The acidity of the one is mitigated by the sweetness of the other, with the pineapple syrup adding a viscous texture to the drink.

1½ measures/6 tsp light rum
1 measure/1½ tbsp red grape juice
1 measure/1½ tbsp passion fruit juice
¼ measure/1 tsp pineapple syrup (from a can)

Shake all the ingredients well with ice, and strain into a rocks glass.

Hustler

This is a sharply tangy drink. I prefer it without sugar to emphasize its bite, but around 5ml/1 tsp will not go amiss, if you find it just too sour without.

1 measure/1½ tbsp light rum
1 measure/1½ tbsp white rum
1 measure/1½ tbsp passion fruit juice
juice of a lime
5ml/1 tsp caster (superfine) sugar (optional)

Shake all the ingredients well with ice (especially well to dissolve the sugar if you are using it), and strain into a large wine goblet. Add the empty shell of the lime to the drink.

Sun City

A similar type of blend to the Mai Tai, and almost as lethal, this is a drink with plenty of personality.

1 measure/1½ tbsp white rum
½ measure/2 tsp dark rum
½ measure/2 tsp Galliano
½ measure/2 tsp apricot brandy
2 measures/3 tbsp pineapple juice
¼ measure/1 tsp lime juice
3 measures/4½ tbsp sparkling lemonade

Shake all but the last ingredient with ice, and then strain into a highball glass. Top up with the lemonade. Garnish with slices of lemon and lime.

Arrowhead

The peachy flavour of Southern Comfort works well with fruity banana and lemon notes in this lightly fizzy rum cocktail.

1 measure/1½ tbsp dark rum
½ measure/2 tsp Southern Comfort
½ measure/2 tsp crème de banane
¼ measure/1 tsp lime juice
3 measures/4½ tbsp sparkling lemonade

Fill a rocks glass with ice nearly to the brim, and then add the ingredients in the order above. Give the drink a gentle stir without dispersing the fizz, and garnish with a half-slice of lemon.

Hurricane

There are almost as many different recipes for a drink called Hurricane as there are cocktail books, but this particular one, with its exuberantly fruity character, is my favourite.

1½ measures/6 tsp dark rum
1 measure/1½ tbsp white rum
1 measure/1½ tbsp lime juice
2 measures/3 tbsp passion fruit juice
1 measure/1½ tbsp pineapple juice
1 measure/1½ tbsp orange juice
½ measure/2 tsp blackcurrant syrup (from
    a can of fruit)

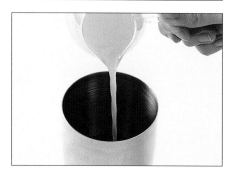

Shake all the ingredients well with ice, and strain into a highball glass. Decorate with slices of pineapple and orange and a cherry.

Chop Nut

An ingenious blend of coconut, chocolate and hazelnut flavours, all sharpened up with orange, this is a most satisfying drink.

1 measure/1½ tbsp white rum
¾ measure/3 tsp Malibu
½ measure/2 tsp white crème de cacao
¼ measure/1 tsp Frangelico
1½ measures/6 tsp mandarin juice

Shake all the ingredients well with ice, and strain into a bowl-shaped cocktail glass. For a slightly frothier texture, add 5ml/1 tsp egg white as well. Garnish with a twist of mandarin rind.

Emerald Star

Despite the presence of the green melon liqueur, the colour of this drink isn't exactly emerald. It's a pretty name nonetheless.

1 measure/1½ tbsp white rum
⅔ measure/1 tbsp Midori
⅓ measure/1½ tsp apricot brandy
⅓ measure/1½ tsp lime juice
1 measure/1½ tbsp passion fruit juice

Shake all the ingredients well with ice, and strain into a cocktail glass. Garnish with a slice of star fruit.

Bartending know-how
When the Japanese melon liqueur, Midori, was launched in New York in 1978, the party was held at the fabled Studio 54 nightclub. John Travolta, who had just made *Grease*, was among the guests.

Eye of the Tiger

This is another drink that has a dark rum float on top. It adds a suitably tigerish bite to what otherwise tastes like a rather innocent fruity mixture.

1 measure/1½ tbsp light rum
1 measure/1½ tbsp Malibu
1 measure/1½ tbsp cranberry juice
1 measure/1½ tbsp lemon juice
1 measure/1½ tbsp orange juice
1 measure/1½ tbsp sugar syrup
½ measure/2 tsp dark rum, preferably
    overproof

Shake all but the last ingredient well with ice, and strain into a highball glass half-filled with cracked ice. Sprinkle the dark rum on to the surface of the drink, and garnish with a slice of orange.

Petite Fleur

This tangy, refreshing cocktail makes a good aperitif. I'm not sure what flower is meant to be invoked by its name. Perhaps you can decide as you drink it.

1 measure/1½ tbsp white rum
1 measure/1½ tbsp Cointreau
1 measure/1½ tbsp grapefruit juice

Shake all the ingredients well with ice, and strain into a cocktail glass. Add a twist of grapefruit rind.

Rompope

Legend has it that this rich egg-nog was first made in the kitchens of a convent in Puebla, Mexico. It is traditional to seal bottles of Rompope with rolled corn husks, or corn cobs that have been stripped of their corn. The recipe makes 1.5 litres/2½ pints, and will keep for up to one week in the refrigerator.

1 litre/1¾ pints milk
350g/12oz sugar
2.5ml/½ tsp bicarbonate of soda (baking soda)
1 cinnamon stick
12 large egg yolks
300ml/½ pint dark rum

Pour the milk into a pan and stir in the sugar and bicarbonate of soda. Add the cinnamon stick. Place the pan over a medium heat and bring the mixture to the boil, stirring constantly. Immediately pour the mixture into a bowl and cool to room temperature. Remove the cinnamon stick, squeezing it gently to release any liquid.

Put the egg yolks in a heatproof bowl over a pan of simmering water and whisk until the mixture is very thick

Yum Yum

The name of this drink is an indication of most people's reactions to this exotically fruity recipe with a fleeting hint of coconut.

1½ measures/6 tsp white rum
½ measure/2 tsp Malibu
1 measure/1½ tbsp mango juice
1 measure/1½ tbsp peach juice
½ measure/2 tsp lime juice

and pale. Add the whisked yolks to the milk mixture a little at a time, beating after each addition.

Return the mixture to a clean pan, place over a low heat and cook until the mixture thickens and the back of the spoon is visible when a finger is drawn along it. Stir in the rum, pour into sterilized bottles and seal tightly with stoppers or clear film (plastic wrap). Chill until required, and serve very cold.

Shake all the ingredients well with ice, and strain into a highball glass half-filled with roughly cracked ice. Garnish with a slice of lime.

Bartending know-how
Malibu is from Jamaica, but its white rum base comes from Barbados.

Poker

Here is a simple cocktail from the 1920s. The preference now is for the proportions given below, although it was originally half-and-half. It may also be made with light rum instead of white, if you prefer.

1½ measures/6 tsp white rum
¾ measure/3 tsp sweet red vermouth

Shake the ingredients well with ice, and strain into a cocktail glass. Squeeze a twist of orange rind over the surface of the drink to release a spray of oil and then drop it in.

Bartending know-how
Recipes based on white rum are far more interesting if made with one of the small producers' island rums, rather than one of the big multi-national proprietary products.

Morning Joy

One wouldn't necessarily recommend making a habit of these, but the idea is of a more robust approach than usual to the glass of breakfast juice. How much joy it spreads over the morning may well depend on how joyful the night before was.

X.Y.Z.

The significance of its mysterious algebraic name escapes me, but this is a 1920s recipe that has survived the test of time. It's a strong one too.

2 measures/3 tbsp dark rum
1 measure/1½ tbsp Cointreau
1 measure/1½ tbsp lemon juice

Shake all the ingredients well with ice, and strain into a large cocktail glass. Add a half-slice of lemon.

1½ measures/6 tsp light rum
6 measures/135ml/4½fl oz grapefruit juice
¼ measure/1 tsp sloe gin

Half-fill a highball glass with cracked ice, and then add the ingredients in this order, sprinkling the sloe gin on top as a float.

Trade Winds

The correct rum brand to use for this cocktail is Mount Gay, made on Barbados. It is properly served frappé.

2 measures/3 tbsp light rum
½ measure/2 tsp slivovitz
½ measure/2 tsp lime juice
½ measure/2 tsp orgeat (almond syrup)

Shake the ingredients well with ice, and strain into a cocktail glass filled with crushed ice. Add a half-slice of lime.

Kingston

This is named after the Jamaican capital, so it would be inappropriate to use rum from any other location.

1½ measures/6 tsp dark Jamaica rum
¾ measure/3 tsp gin
juice of half a lime
¼ measure/1 tsp grenadine

Shake all the ingredients well with ice, and strain into a cocktail glass. Garnish with a half-slice of lime.

Continental

An old-fashioned mixture of rum and peppermint cordial was once a popular drink. This cocktail presents a more adventurous spin on that formula. The colour is an attractive shade of tawny, and the mint flavour is agreeably set off by the piercing note of lime.

1½ measures/6 tsp light rum
½ measure/2 tsp green crème de menthe
½ measure/2 tsp lime juice

Shake all the ingredients well with ice, and strain into a cocktail glass. If available, add a sprig of mint to the drink.

Bolero

Here is one of those cocktails that's all alcohol and no mixers. Stirring the drink gently, as opposed to shaking it, emphasizes its strength, in the sense that the mixture doesn't become quite as chilled as it would in the shaker.

1½ measures/6 tsp light rum
¾ measure/3 tsp calvados
¼ measure/1 tsp sweet red vermouth

Mix the ingredients gently in a pitcher with a couple of ice cubes, and then strain into a pre-chilled rocks glass. Squeeze a twist of lemon over the drink, and then drop it in.

Pilot Boat

With its mixture of dark rum and banana, this is the most tropical-tasting cocktail imaginable. The relatively high proportion of citrus helps to sharpen it up most agreeably.

1½ measures/6 tsp dark rum, preferably Jamaica
1 measure/1½ tbsp crème de banane
2 measures/3 tbsp lemon juice

Shake all the ingredients well with ice, and strain into a bowl-shaped cocktail glass. Garnish with a slice of lemon.

Whisky

It is perhaps whisky that is the trickiest base ingredient to use in cocktails. Its flavour doesn't take quite as obligingly as the other spirits do to being mixed with liqueurs and fruit juices, although it is by no means bereft of its classic recipes. The rich, sweetly woody flavours of American whiskeys such as bourbon and rye, and the fruitiness of Canadian whisky, are better in this respect than Scotch. It is the iodiney pungency of much single malt Scotch that gets in the way. Perhaps these products really are best enjoyed on their own, or else with nothing more elaborate than fresh spring water.

Whisky Sour

Mix the juice of half a lemon with 5ml/ 1 tsp caster (superfine) sugar in a small tumbler with two or three cubes of ice. When the sugar is dissolved, add a generous measure of whisky and stir again – American whiskeys are best for this preparation. Some people add a brief squirt of soda. If you find this formula a little too sour, add a little more sugar, but this is the way I like it.

Perfect Manhattan

When making Manhattans it's a matter of preference whether you use sweet vermouth, dry vermouth or a mixture of the two. Both of the former require a dash of Angostura bitters. The last, given here, is such a harmoniously balanced mixture that it doesn't need it.

2 measures/3 tbsp rye whiskey
¼ measure/1 tsp dry vermouth
¼ measure/1 tsp sweet red vermouth

Pour the whiskey and vermouths into a bar glass half-full of ice. Stir well for 30 seconds to mix and chill. Strain on the rocks or straight up into a chilled cocktail glass. Pare away a small strip of lemon rind. Tie it into a knot to help release the oils from the rind, and drop it into the cocktail. Add a maraschino cherry with its stalk left intact. As any Manhattan drinker wil tell you, the cherry is essential.

Rob Roy

A further modification of the Perfect Manhattan recipe, Rob Roy is made with Scotch, and inclines very much to the sweeter end of the spectrum. It has traditionally been drunk on St Andrew's Day, November 30, but may with confidence be drunk all year round now.

1 measure/1½ tbsp Scotch
1 measure/1½ tbsp sweet red vermouth

Shake the ingredients well with ice, and strain into a cocktail glass. Some recipes add a dash of Angostura bitters to the mix as well, but I leave that to your discretion.

Mint Julep

One of the oldest cocktails of them all, this originated in the southern states of the USA, probably in the 18th century. It's the drink of tradition at the Kentucky Derby, the first Saturday in May, and is an incomparably refreshing mixture that has deservedly become a classic.

15ml/1 tbsp caster (superfine) sugar
8–10 fresh mint leaves
⅔ measure/1 tbsp hot water
2 measures/3 tbsp bourbon

Place the sugar in a mortar or bar glass. Tear the mint leaves into small pieces and add them to the sugar. Bruise them with a pestle or use a muddler to release their flavour and colour. Add the hot water and grind well together. Spoon into a highball glass and half-fill with crushed ice. Add the bourbon.

Stir until the outside of the glass has frosted. Allow to stand for a couple of minutes until the ice melts slightly and dilutes the drink.

Whisky Mac

The classic cold remedy is half-and-half good Scotch and green ginger wine (preferably Crabbie's). These days, it is generally served over ice in a rocks glass, but traditionally it was taken straight up. Whether it actually gets rid of a cold must be open to doubt, but it certainly makes you feel better.

Canada Cocktail

An engagingly sweet and fruity cocktail that obviously has to be made with whisky from Canada. Canadian Club is a fine brand, and is generally available.

1½ measures/6 tsp Canadian whisky
¼ measure/1 tsp Cointreau
2 dashes Angostura bitters
5ml/1 tsp caster (superfine) sugar

Shake all the ingredients well with ice, and strain into a cocktail glass. Garnish with a twist of orange rind.

Bobby Burns

Similar to Rob Roy, but with the herbal tang of Bénédictine coming through it, this is a drink named after Scotland's national poet. It is best served on Burns Night, January 25.

1½ measures/6 tsp Scotch
¾ measure/3 tsp sweet red vermouth
¼ measure/1 tsp Bénédictine

Stir all the ingredients well with ice, and strain into a chilled cocktail glass. Squeeze a spray of oil from a piece of lemon rind over the surface, but in this case don't add the rind to the drink. In the 1920s, the cocktail was shaken, but it seems to work better stirred, which gives a less cloudy result.

Old-Fashioned

The Old-Fashioned is only a modified bourbon or rye whiskey, but quickly established itself as one of the all-time classic preparations. It is usually heavily garnished, and served in a particular kind of squat tumbler that is named after the drink.

¼ measure/1 tsp sugar syrup
2 dashes Angostura bitters
2 measures/3 tbsp bourbon or rye whiskey

Mix the sugar and Angostura in an Old-Fashioned glass until the sugar is dissolved. Add plenty of cracked ice and then the whiskey. Throw in a twist of lemon rind, a slice of orange cut laterally from the fruit and a cocktail cherry, and serve with a stirring implement
in it. This is the most old-fashioned formula for an Old-Fashioned.

New York

This is another simple preparation for whisky that was made in the 1920s with Canadian whisky, despite its name. Scotch can also successfully be used, however, as can, seemingly, anything but American whiskey.

2 measures/3 tbsp Canadian whisky or
  Scotch
5ml/1 tsp caster (superfine) sugar
juice of half a lime
dash grenadine

Stir all the ingredients vigorously with ice in a pitcher, and then strain into a chilled cocktail glass. Squeeze a twist of lemon over the drink, but don't drop it in.

Bartending know-how
Bourbon and rye whiskeys have quite distinctive flavours. In each case, the chosen grain must constitute at least 51% of the mash (corn being used in bourbon). Rye results in a thicker, heavier-tasting whiskey with a rather more rustic appeal than classic bourbon.

Rusty Nail

A short, sharp drink, this is another classic half-and-half recipe, and one that still manages to do perfect justice to both ingredients.

1½ measures/6 tsp Scotch
1½ measures/6 tsp Drambuie

Pour both ingredients over crushed ice in a rocks glass or whisky tumbler, and stir gently. No garnish is necessary. Some prefer to leave the ice cubes whole so as not to dilute the drink too much. It should be drunk quickly.

Bartending know-how
A Rusty Nail is really *the* Drambuie cocktail. Attempts to make this fine Scottish liqueur blend with anything other than Scotch always seem to come to grief. It genuinely seems to be too good to mix.

Sea Dog

This is a long Scotch whisky drink with a citrus twist. For a sweeter drink, add a second sugar cube.

1–2 sugar cubes
2 dashes Angostura bitters
2 orange wedges
2 lemon wedges
⅔ measure/1 tbsp Scotch
1 measure/1½ tbsp Bénédictine
2 measures/3 tbsp soda water

Put the sugar cube at the bottom of a highball glass, add the bitters and allow to soak into the sugar cube. Add the orange and lemon wedges and, using a muddler, press the juices from the fruit. Fill the glass with cracked ice. Add the whisky and Bénédictine, and mix together well with a swizzle-stick. Add the chilled soda water. Serve with the muddler, so that more juice can be pressed from the fruit by the drinker. Garnish with a maraschino cherry.

Gall Bracer

Short and smart, this drink is served on the rocks in a tumbler, or in a long-stemmed glass with a maraschino cherry. It all depends on the drinker and the occasion.

2 dashes Angostura bitters
2 dashes grenadine
2 measures/3 tbsp bourbon or rye whiskey

Millionaire

Several cocktails have been recorded over the years under this name. The *Savoy Cocktail Book* lists two alternatives, one based on rum, the other on gin. This one is from roughly the same era, though.

1½ measures/6 tsp bourbon
¾ measure/3 tsp Cointreau
dash grenadine
½ egg white

Shake all the ingredients well with ice, and strain into a cocktail glass. Garnish with a half-slice of lemon.

Half-fill a bar glass with ice cubes. Add the Angostura bitters, grenadine and whiskey, and stir well to chill. Place some ice in a small tumbler and pour the cocktail over it. Squeeze lemon rind over the top and then discard. Garnish with a cherry, if desired. For a longer drink, finish with soda or sparkling mineral water.

Buckaroo

Not many cocktails work well with cola, but this is an honourable exception. The pronounced bittering note contributed by the Angostura is essential and should not be omitted.

1½ measures/6 tsp bourbon
2.5ml/½ tsp Angostura bitters
5 measures/120ml/4fl oz Coca-Cola

Add the first two ingredients to a highball glass containing plenty of cracked ice. Stir briskly and then top up with cola. Serve with a swizzle-stick for further stirring.

Pleasant Dreams

This fruity treatment for bourbon would make a very comforting nightcap – so long as you confine yourself to just the one, that is.

1½ measures/6 tsp bourbon
¾ measure/3 tsp crème de mûre
¼ measure/1 tsp peach schnapps

Shake all the ingredients well with ice, and pour without straining into a chilled rocks glass.

Artists' Special

This drink is so-named because it was invented at the Artists' Club in the rue Pigalle, Paris, in the 1920s. The red ingredient was originally redcurrant syrup, but grenadine can be used to perfectly good effect instead. The mixture of Scotch and sweet sherry at its heart is a very appealing one.

1 measure/1½ tbsp Scotch
1 measure/1½ tbsp sweet brown sherry
½ measure/2 tsp lemon juice
½ measure/2 tsp grenadine

Shake all the ingredients well with ice, and strain into a cocktail glass. Add a half-slice of lemon.

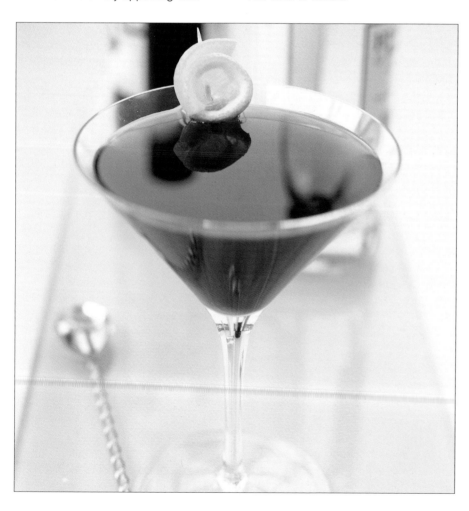

Algonquin

This is named after the elegant New York hotel where Dorothy Parker once ruled the roost. The types of whisky to be used are once again quite specific.

2 measures/3 tbsp rye or Canadian whisky
1 measure/1½ tbsp dry vermouth
1 measure/1½ tbsp pineapple juice

Shake all the ingredients well with ice, and strain into a rocks glass half-filled with cracked ice. Garnish with lemon.

Pamplemousse

The name is the French word for "grapefruit", and so it's not hard to work out what the principal flavour of this charming cocktail should be.

1½ measures/6 tsp Canadian whisky
½ measure/2 tsp Southern Comfort
2 measures/3 tbsp grapefruit juice
¼ measure/1 tsp pineapple syrup

Shake all the ingredients well with ice, and then strain into a rocks glass half-filled with cracked ice. Add a short twist of grapefruit rind and a cocktail cherry.

Bartending know-how
Both Canadian whisky and Southern Comfort have a pronounced fruity flavour, the latter derived at least partly from the use of peaches. They work particularly well in fruity mixtures such as this one.

Rocky Mountain

Here is another of those cocktails that calls for three specific brands, and wouldn't be quite the same with substitutes. Its light, delicately herbal tinge is very attractive.

1½ measures/6 tsp Canadian Club
½ measure/2 tsp Glayva
¼ measure/1 tsp Punt e Mes

Shake all the ingredients well with ice, and pour without straining into a chilled rocks glass.

Bartending know-how
The Italian aperitif Punt e Mes, created in Turin in 1870, contains around four dozen herbs and spices on a white wine base. In Italy, it is traditionally accompanied by a piece of strong, dark chocolate.

Blizzard

The trick with this drink is to shake it for longer than normal with masses of ice until the mixture is extremely frosty-looking. That incidentally goes some way to disguise the high proportion of bourbon in it.

3 measures/4½ tbsp bourbon
1 measure/1½ tbsp cranberry juice

Grenoble

This is a superbly fruity cocktail with quite a kick, and one that demonstrates what a good mixer Kentucky whiskey is.

1½ measures/6 tsp bourbon
½ measure/2 tsp crème de framboise
½ measure/2 tsp Cointreau
1 measure/1½ tbsp orange juice
¼ measure/1 tsp orgeat syrup

Shake all the ingredients well with ice, and strain into a cocktail glass. Garnish with a half-slice of orange and a raspberry on a cocktail stick.

⅔ measure/1 tbsp lemon juice
30ml/2 tbsp sugar syrup

Shake all the ingredients extremely well with plenty of large ice cubes, and pour the mixture unstrained into a chilled highball glass. Garnish with a slice of lemon, and perhaps a couple of cranberries.

Tivoli

There is an Italian connection in this powerful little cocktail to reflect its name, but it comes by way of Scandinavia and Kentucky.

1½ measures/6 tsp bourbon
½ measure/2 tsp sweet red vermouth
½ measure/2 tsp aquavit
dash Campari

Shake all the ingredients well with ice, and strain into a chilled cocktail glass. Garnish the drink with a half-slice of lemon.

Paddy

Another traditional one, this was originally made with the Irish whiskey brand of the same name. In the 1920s, it had equal quantities of whiskey and vermouth and slightly less Angostura, which would obviously make for a sweeter result. This is today's drier and more sophisticated formula.

1½ measures/6 tsp Irish whiskey
¾ measure/3 tsp sweet red vermouth
3 dashes Angostura bitters

Shake all the ingredients well with ice, and strain into a chilled cocktail glass. Garnish with a half-slice of lemon.

Highland Morning

Tipperary

You'll certainly know you've had one of these! Tipperary is an old 1920s mixture that's all alcohol, and packs the considerable punch of Chartreuse. If you're feeling brave, the Chartreuse was originally a whole measure too.

1 measure/1½ tbsp Irish whiskey
1 measure/1½ tbsp sweet red vermouth
½ measure/2 tsp green Chartreuse

Add the ingredients to a pitcher with plenty of cracked ice, and stir until cold enough to frost the sides of the glass. Strain into a pre-chilled cocktail glass.

Although the name seems to be encouraging you to drink one of these for breakfast, a little later in the day might be wiser.

1 measure/1½ tbsp Scotch
¾ measure/3 tsp Cointreau
3 measures/4½ tbsp grapefruit juice

Loch Ness

A pair of Scottish and a pair of Irish cocktails rounds off with this tough cookie, which dates from the 1920s.

1½ measures/6 tsp Scotch
1 measure/1½ tbsp Pernod

Shake all the ingredients well with ice, and pour (unstrained if you really are having it in the morning) into a chilled rocks glass. The drink could be garnished with a twist of grapefruit rind and perhaps a half-slice of orange to reflect the presence of Cointreau in the mix.

¼ measure/1 tsp sweet red vermouth

Shake all the ingredients well with ice, and pour without straining into a chilled rocks glass or Old-Fashioned glass. Do not garnish.

Coffee Egg-Nog

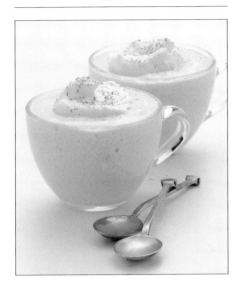

This is a rather special coffee drink, particularly suitable for daytime summer-holiday festivities. The recipe serves six to eight.

8 eggs, separated
225g/8oz sugar
250ml/8fl oz cold strong coffee (espresso strength or filter/cafetière brewed at 75g/3oz coffee per 1 litre/1¾ pints water)
220ml/7½fl oz Scotch or bourbon
220ml/7½fl oz double (heavy) cream
120ml/4fl oz whipped cream
ground nutmeg, to decorate

Thoroughly beat the egg yolks, then add the sugar, mixing well. Heat gently in a pan over a low heat, stirring with a wooden spoon. Allow to cool a few minutes, stir in the coffee and whisky, and then slowly add the cream, stirring well. Beat the egg whites until stiff and stir into the egg-nog, mixing well. Pour into small round cups, top each with a small dollop of whipped cream and sprinkle nutmeg on top.

Jamaica Shake

Combining the best of both worlds, this cream cocktail brings together the complementary richnesses of American whiskey and Jamaica rum. It's a milkshake for adults.

1½ measures/6 tsp bourbon
1 measure/1½ tbsp dark Jamaica rum
1 measure/1½ tbsp double (heavy) cream

Shake all the ingredients well with ice to amalgamate the cream, and strain into a cocktail glass. Sift grated chocolate over the top.

Irish Chocolate Velvet

This is a luxurious creamy hot chocolate drink, with just a touch of alcohol to fortify it. It would be the perfect antidote to a winter morning spent working outdoors. The recipe serves four.

250ml/8fl oz double (heavy) cream
400ml/14fl oz milk
115g/4oz milk chocolate, chopped into small pieces
30ml/2 tbsp cocoa powder
60ml/4 tbsp Irish whiskey
whipped cream, for topping

Ring of Kerry

Since Irish whiskey lends itself so well to these creamy treatments, here is another one, in which it appears with its much-loved compatriot, Bailey's Irish Cream.

1½ measures/6 tsp Irish whiskey
1 measure/1½ tbsp Bailey's Irish Cream
½ measure/2 tsp Kahlúa

Shake all the ingredients well with ice, and strain into a chilled cocktail glass. Sprinkle 5ml/1 tsp grated chocolate over the top.

Whip half the cream in a bowl until it is thick enough to hold its shape. Place the milk and chocolate in a pan and heat gently, stirring, until the chocolate has melted. Whisk in the cocoa, then bring to the boil. Remove from the heat and stir in the remaining cream and the Irish whiskey. Pour quickly into four warmed heatproof mugs or glasses and top each serving with a generous spoonful of the whipped cream, finishing with a garnish of milk chocolate curls.

Tequila

Being even more of a recent commercial phenomenon than vodka, tequila has acquired correspondingly fewer recipes so far in the cocktail repertoire. That is gradually changing on modern bar menus as the salty, savoury, slightly feral aroma and flavour of the drink are appreciated. It mixes well with most fruit juices, and although combinations with liqueurs are still only at a fairly tentative stage, they are developing. There is therefore an experimental quality to some of the recipes that follow. Don't forget that, as well as basic, so-called "silver" tequila, there is also the richer and more complex oro, or "gold", style that has been aged in wooden casks.

Tequila Sunrise

This classic Mexican recipe of the 1930s takes its name from the way the grenadine – that bright red pomegranate cordial – first sinks in the glass of orange juice and then rises to the surface. Add it too slowly and it will simply blend into the drink, turning it a fetching (but totally incorrect) scarlet colour.

2 measures/3 tbsp gold tequila
4 measures/6 tbsp freshly squeezed orange
   juice
½ measure/2 tsp grenadine

Half-fill a highball glass with crushed ice. Pour in the tequila, then the orange juice, which must be freshly squeezed. Quickly add the grenadine, pouring it down the back of a spoon held inside the glass so that it sinks to the bottom of the drink. You could garnish the drink with a slice of orange and a cherry.

Tequila Sunset

This variation on the popular party drink can be mixed and chilled in a pitcher, ready to pour into glasses, and finished at the last minute with the addition of crème de cassis and honey.

1 measure/1½ tbsp gold tequila
5 measures/120ml/4fl oz lemon juice
1 measure/1½ tbsp orange juice
15–30ml/1–2 tbsp clear honey
⅔ measure/1 tbsp crème de cassis

Pour the tequila, and lemon and orange juices into a well-chilled cocktail glass. Using a swizzle-stick, mix the ingredients together well. Trickle the honey into the centre of the drink. It will sink and create a layer at the bottom of the glass. Add the crème de cassis, but do not stir. It will create a glowing layer above the honey at the bottom of the glass.

Margarita

With the Tequila Sunrise, Margarita (created in Tijuana in the late 1940s) is probably the best-known tequila cocktail of them all, and these days is a sight more popular. Its saltiness and sourness make it a great aperitif, and it is pleasingly strong too. Some recipes use lemon juice instead of lime, but lime juice sharpens its bite.

1½ measures/6 tsp silver tequila
½ measure/2 tsp Cointreau
juice of a lime

Rub the rim of a cocktail glass with a wedge of fresh lime, and then dip it in fine salt. Shake the tequila, Cointreau and lime juice with plenty of ice, and strain into the prepared glass. Garnish with a twist of cucumber rind or a half-slice of lime.

Iced Margarita

This smooth sorbet drink has all the punch of Mexico's renowned cocktail. This recipe makes two drinks.

2½ measures/3½ tbsp silver tequila
1¼ measures/5½ tsp Cointreau
1¼ measures/5½ tsp lime juice
6–8 small scoops lime sorbet
150ml/¼ pint chilled lemonade

Frost the rims of the glasses with cut lime and caster (superfine) sugar. Add lime and lemon slices to each. Mix the tequila, Cointreau and lime juice in a jug. Scoop the sorbet into the glasses. Pour an equal quantity of the drink into each glass. Top with lemonade and garnish with lemon balm.

Mango and Peach Margarita

Adding puréed fruit to the classic tequila mixture alters the consistency. This recipe serves four.

2 mangoes, peeled and sliced
3 peaches, peeled and sliced
5 measures/120ml/4fl oz silver tequila
2½ measures/3½ tbsp Cointreau
2½ measures/3½ tbsp lime juice

Blend the mango and peach slices in a liquidizer until a smooth paste is obtained. Add the tequila, Cointreau and lime juice, blend for a few seconds more, then add the ice. Blend again until the drink has the consistency of a milkshake. Pour into pre-chilled cocktail glasses, and garnish with slices of mango with the skin left on. Create other fruit variations on the basic Margarita, using this recipe.

Cactus Juice

In this modern recipe, the roundness of flavour of gold tequila is enhanced by marrying it with a little of the herb-flavoured Scotch liqueur, Drambuie.

2 measures/3 tbsp gold tequila
¼ measure/1 tsp Drambuie
1 measure/1½ tbsp lemon juice
5ml/1 tsp caster (superfine) sugar

Shake all the ingredients well with ice until the sugar is dissolved, and pour without straining into a rocks glass. Add a slice of lemon.

Pineapple Tequila

Flavours such as almond and quince have been added to silver tequila for some time. Many bars have developed unique flavours by combining ingredients such as chillies with tequila, and leaving them to infuse. The method below will make a smooth, fruity drink to serve six.

1 large pineapple
50g/2oz soft dark brown sugar
1 litre/1¾ pints silver tequila
1 vanilla pod

Rinse a large (about 2 litre/3½ pint) wide-necked bottle or demijohn and sterilize by placing it in an oven and then

turning on the oven and setting it at 110°C/225°F/Gas ¼. After 20 minutes remove the bottle from the oven with oven gloves and allow it to cool down.

Cut the top off the pineapple and then cut away the skin. Cut the flesh in half lengthways, then remove the hard centre core and discard it. Chop the rest of the pineapple into chunks, ensuring that they are small enough to fit in the bottle neck.

When the bottle is completely cold, put the pineapple into the bottle. Mix the sugar and tequila together in a pitcher until the sugar dissolves and then pour into the bottle. Split the vanilla pod and add it to the rest of the ingredients.

Gently agitate the bottle a few times each day to stir the contents. Allow the tequila to stand for at least a week before drinking with ice. (When all the tequila has been drunk, use the pineapple in desserts such as ice cream, or warm with butter and cinnamon and serve with cream.)

Home infusions of tequila like this are very popular in its native Mexico.

TNT

With a bit of twisting, the initials of the name just about indicate the ingredients of the drink: tequila, Napoléon and Tia (Maria). Rather more accurately, they mirror the effect of the drink, which is all alcohol with no mixers. The flavour is very satisfying, though.

1 measure/1½ tbsp gold tequila
½ measure Mandarine Napoléon
1 measure/1½ tbsp Tia Maria

Stir all the ingredients gently with ice in a pitcher until very cold, and then strain into a rocks glass half-filled with cracked ice. Suspend a twist of orange rind in the drink.

Tequila and Orange

Have done with the lemon-squeezing and salt-licking fuss associated with traditional tequila-drinking, and try tequila on the rocks with fresh orange juice and a half-slice of orange. It makes an enlivening change for those grown weary of vodka-and-orange. Silver tequila will do for this mix.

Mexican Chocolate

A chillier, and more inspiring, version of boozy hot chocolate, this makes a refreshingly original drink for a hot summer afternoon. It beats chocolate ice cream, anyway.

1½ measures/6 tsp gold tequila
1 measure/1½ tbsp Kahlúa
4 measures/6 tbsp prepared cocoa or drinking chocolate, made with full-cream (whole) milk

Shake all the ingredients well with ice, and strain into a large goblet. Drink through straws.

Tequila Slammer

The Slammer reflects something of the bravado with which tequila is traditionally drunk in Mexico. It is a drink in which one takes over the bartender's performance ethic for oneself, and it has not surprisingly become internationally practised among a certain age group.

1 measure/1½ tbsp silver or gold tequila
1 measure/1½ tbsp sparkling mixer (usually either lemonade or ginger ale, but can be sparkling wine)

Pour the two measures into a shot glass, cover with the palm of your hand (or a beer mat, if you don't fancy getting messy) and slam the glass down a couple of times on the bar counter. The drink will then fizz wildly up, and you have something less than a second to get it to your mouth, and down it in one.

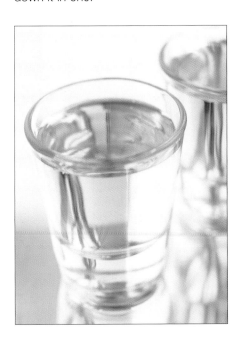

Bloody Maria

A close cousin of the original vodka-based Bloody Mary, this simple cocktail consists of tequila and tomato juice mixed together with spicy seasonings. The quantities here make two drinks, just in case that hangover is particularly persistent, or you have a fellow sufferer.

Bar Bandit

A long, fruity drink with a subtle, but nonetheless recognizable punch behind it. The inclusion of both types of vermouth proves once again the versatility of this style of fortified wine.

1 measure/1½ tbsp gold tequila
½ measure/2 tsp dry vermouth
½ measure/2 tsp sweet red vermouth
½ measure/2 tsp crème de framboise
¼ measure/1 tsp lime juice
4 measures/6 tbsp sparkling cherryade

Pack a highball glass with cracked ice, and add all but the last ingredient in the order above. Stir briskly with a swizzle-stick, and then top up with cherryade. Garnish with a slice of lime and a couple of cocktail cherries.

250ml/8fl oz tomato juice, chilled
2 measures/3 tbsp silver tequila
5ml/1 tsp Worcestershire sauce
few drops Tabasco
juice of half a lemon
pinch celery salt
salt and freshly ground black pepper

Pour the chilled tomato juice into a large pitcher and stir in the tequila. Add the Worcestershire sauce and stir the mixture well. Add a few drops of Tabasco and the lemon juice. Taste and season with celery salt, salt and pepper. Serve over ice cubes in highball glasses, with celery sticks standing in the drink for stirring it. The tequila naturally makes its presence felt in this mixture more obviously than vodka does.

Boomer

This is one of those recently popular drinks known as shooters, which are small, assertively flavoured preparations for downing at one gulp. It should be served either in a shot glass or small liqueur glass, when its short, sharp shock can be best appreciated.

⅔ measure/1 tbsp gold tequila
½ measure/2 tsp apricot brandy
½ measure/2 tsp orange juice
¼ measure/1 tsp lemon juice
¼ measure/1 tsp sugar syrup

Shake all the ingredients well with ice, and strain into a tiny glass.

Firebird

This is a fairly sweet, fizzy concoction that's shorter than most other sparkling cocktails.

1½ measures/6 tsp silver tequila
½ measure/2 tsp crème de banane
½ measure/2 tsp lime juice
2 measures/3 tbsp sparkling lemonade

Fill a rocks glass nearly to the brim with cracked ice. Add the first three ingredients, give them a quick stir and then add the lemonade. Garnish with a slice of lemon.

Sangrita

Sipping sangrita and tequila alternately is a taste sensation not to be missed, the warm flavours of the first balancing the strength of the second. The drinks are often served with *antojitos* (nibbles) as an appetizer. This recipe serves eight.

450g/1lb ripe tomatoes, or one 400g/14oz can chopped tomatoes
1 small onion, finely chopped
2 small fresh green chillies, seeded and chopped
120ml/4fl oz freshly squeezed orange juice
juice of 3 limes
2.5ml/½ tsp caster (superfine) sugar
pinch of salt
1 small shot glass gold or aged tequila per person

Cut a large cross in the base of each tomato. Place the tomatoes in a heatproof bowl and pour over boiling water to cover. Leave for 3 minutes. Lift the tomatoes out on a slotted spoon, and plunge them into a second bowl of cold water. Remove the skins, then cut the tomatoes in half and scoop out the seeds with a spoon. Chop the tomato flesh and put in a food processor. Add the onion, chillies, orange juice, lime juice, sugar and salt. Process until all the mixture is very smooth, then pour into a pitcher and chill for at least an hour before serving. Offer each drinker a separate shot glass of neat tequila as well. The drinks are sipped alternately.

Last Chance

A drop of honey makes a good companion for mellow, cask-aged tequila in this drink. It would make a rather comforting nightcap.

1¾ measures/2½ tbsp gold tequila
½ measure/1 tsp apricot brandy
1 measure/1½ tbsp lime juice
10ml/2 tsp clear honey

Shake all the ingredients very well with ice, ensuring that the honey is fully dissolved, and strain into a rocks glass. Garnish with a slice of lime.

Cherry Coco

Here is a sumptuously creamy, exotically flavoured cocktail that would look very elegant served in a champagne flute. It's both creamy and sour – a nice combination.

1½ measures/6 tsp silver tequila
¾ measure/3 tsp coconut cream
1 measure/1¼ tbsp lemon juice
¼ measure/1 tsp maraschino

Shake all the ingredients well with ice, and strain into a tall, narrow glass. Drop a cocktail cherry into the drink.

Zorro

John J. Poister, author of *The New American Bartender's Guide*, has created this winning tequila recipe that uses the Balkan plum spirit, slivovitz.

1½ measures/6 tsp silver tequila
1 measure/1½ tbsp slivovitz
1 measure/1½ tbsp lime juice
¼ measure/1 tsp sugar syrup

Shake all the ingredients well with ice, and strain into a chilled cocktail glass. You could garnish with a slice of lime.

Bartending know-how
The best brands of slivovitz hail from Bosnia, Croatia and Serbia, and are made with a local plum variety called pozega, sourced from trees with a minimum age of 20 years.

Piñata

An odd name this, as you might think it contained pineapple, but no – banana and lime are the fruit flavours. It is, nonetheless, quite delicious enough to be going on with.

1½ measures/6 tsp gold tequila
1 measure/1½ tbsp crème de banane
1 measure/1½ tbsp lime juice

Shake all the ingredients well with ice, and strain into a cocktail glass. Dangle a twist of lime rind in the drink.

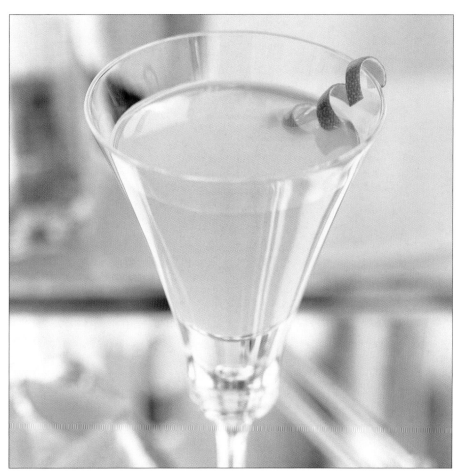

Rosita

A drink that bears some distant kinship to the Negroni, and is prepared in roughly the same way.

1½ measures/6 tsp silver tequila
1 measure/1½ tbsp Campari
½ measure/2 tsp dry vermouth
½ measure/2 tsp sweet red vermouth

Add the ingredients in this order to an Old-Fashioned glass or small rocks glass, half-filled with cracked ice. Stir. Squeeze a small twist of orange rind over the drink and then drop it in.

Mockingbird

A good balance of sweet and sour is achieved in this minty, but sharp-edged cocktail. It's one of those tastes of which one can say that a little goes a long way.

1½ measures/6 tsp silver tequila
¾ measure/3 tsp white crème de menthe
juice of half a lime

Shake all the ingredients well with ice, and strain into a chilled cocktail glass. Garnish with a half-slice of lime and a sprig of mint.

Brandy

In his strange, single-gendered world, Dr Johnson was quite clear about the status of brandy: "Claret is the liquor for boys; port for men; but he who aspires to be a hero must drink brandy." Indeed, fine cognac has for a long time been associated with a certain swaggering demeanour. Not for nothing is one of the top grades of cognac called Napoleon brandy. As well as cognac, there is armagnac from the south-west of France, and brandies from Spain, Germany, Mexico and the USA. They are good mixers in cocktails, and although, understandably, you wouldn't want to use your best Fine Champagne cognac in a mixed drink, it pays not to go for the cheapest grades either. They largely taste horrible, and will ruin the resulting cocktail.

Brandy Cocktail

Over time, this drink became modified to include Cointreau instead of curaçao, a little sugar syrup and a dash of Angostura. However, the earliest versions of it are nothing more than cognac with a soupçon of bitterness.

1½ measures/6 tsp cognac
2 dashes orange curaçao

Stir the ingredients gently with ice in a bar glass, and then strain into a brandy balloon. Do not garnish.

Brandy Fix

A Fix is a mixture of spirit with lemon juice, sweetening and in this case another alcohol flavour, with the shell of the lemon and a pile of ice left in the drink for good measure.

5ml/1 tsp sugar
juice and rind of half a lemon

1½ measures/6 tsp cognac
¾ measure/3 tsp cherry brandy

Dissolve the sugar in a little water in the bottom of a small tumbler, and then fill it with crushed ice. Add the lemon juice and alcohol and stir the drink well. Drop in the squeezed lemon rind.

Bonnie Prince Charlie

As its name indicates, this drink contains Drambuie, the liqueur that was given to Prince Charlie by the MacDonald family on his flight to Skye. The mixture is a strong one, but one that seems to do justice to the liqueur.

1 measure/1½ tbsp cognac
½ measure/2 tsp Drambuie
1 measure/1½ tbsp lemon juice

Shake all the ingredients well with ice, and strain into a cocktail glass. Garnish with a twist of lemon.

Brandy Blazer

A warming after-dinner tipple, this is ideally served with fresh vanilla ice cream or caramelized oranges.

½ orange
1 lemon
2 measures/3 tbsp cognac
1 sugar cube
½ measure/2 tsp Kahlúa

Pare the rind from the orange and lemon, removing and discarding as much of the white pith as possible. Put the cognac, sugar cube, lemon and orange rind in a small pan. Heat gently, then remove from the heat, light a match and pass the flame close to the surface of the liquid. The alcohol will burn with a low, blue flame for about a minute. Blow out the flame. Add the Kahlúa to the pan, and strain into a heat-resistant glass. Garnish with a cocktail stick threaded with orange rind, and serve warm.

B&B

The traditional mix of this world-famous cocktail is half-and-half Bénédictine and good brandy (cognac for preference), stirred not shaken, and not usually iced. In fact, for true authenticity, you don't even need a stirrer. The two drinks are simply poured into a balloon glass, the brandy first, and the drink swirled in the hand before being passed to its recipient. No garnish is needed.

Brandy Smash

The excitingly named Smash is essentially a miniaturized julep (or Mint Julep). It may be made with any spirit, but is particularly successful with brandy.

5ml/1 tsp caster (superfine) sugar
4 mint leaves
2 measures/3 tbsp cognac
1 measure/1½ tbsp soda water

Dissolve the sugar in a little water in a tumbler. Add the mint leaves and press them into the sugar solution to express some of the juices. Put in a couple of ice cubes, and then add the brandy and stir vigorously. Add the soda. Squeeze a piece of lemon rind over the top of the drink, and decorate with a half-slice of orange.

Brandy Crusta

The sweet, frosted rim is all-important in this most appealing drink. It mitigates some of the sourness in the drink itself.

1½ measures/6 tsp cognac
½ measure/2 tsp Cointreau
¼ measure/1 tsp maraschino
dash Angostura bitters
¼ measure/1 tsp lemon juice

Frost the rim of a wide tumbler by dipping it first in lemon juice and then in caster (superfine) sugar. Hang a twist of lemon rind in it, and then fill it with cracked ice. Stir all the ingredients well with ice in a pitcher until the mixture is well-chilled, and then strain into the prepared glass. Garnish further with a half-slice of orange.

Brandy Alexander

One of the greatest cocktails of them all, Alexander can be served at the end of a grand dinner with coffee as a creamy digestif, or as the first drink of the evening at a cocktail party, since the cream in it helps to line the stomach. It was possibly originally made with gin rather than brandy, and the cream was sweetened, but the formula below is undoubtedly the best of all possible worlds.

1 measure/1½ tbsp cognac
1 measure/1½ tbsp brown crème de cacao
1 measure/1½ tbsp double (heavy) cream

Shake the ingredients thoroughly with ice, and strain into a cocktail glass. Scatter ground nutmeg, or grate a little whole nutmeg, on top. Alternatively, sprinkle with grated dark chocolate.

Corpse Reviver 1

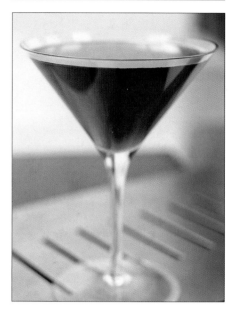

Not the most delicately named cocktail, this is a 1970s recipe intended of course as a morning-after remedy. I'm not sure I'd make quite that claim for it myself, but in its bitterly minty way, it tastes convincingly medicinal, which is what matters.

1 measure/1½ tbsp cognac
1 measure/1½ tbsp Fernet Branca
1 measure/1½ tbsp white crème de menthe

Shake all the ingredients well with ice, and strain into a cocktail glass. Do not garnish. If you really are taking it at 10 o'clock in the morning, you're not likely to care about twists of this and slices of that anyway.

Corpse Reviver 2

This was the 1920s idea of a morning-after remedy, and is probably the first recipe that can lay claim to this name. It looks much more like a night-before drink to me – and a good one at that.

1½ measures/6 tsp cognac
¾ measure/3 tsp calvados
¾ measure/3 tsp sweet red vermouth

Shake all the ingredients well with ice, and strain into a cocktail glass. Again, no garnish is required.

Morning Glory Fizz

A good early-morning drink, this should be consumed as soon as it is made, before it loses its bubbles.

⅔ measure/1 tbsp cognac
¼ measure/1 tsp orange curaçao
¼ measure/1 tsp lemon juice
dash anisette
2 dashes Angostura bitters
4 measures/6 tbsp soda water

Shake all but the last ingredient well with ice, and strain into a chilled highball glass. Finish with the soda water. Garnish the drink with a twist of lemon rind.

Bartending know-how
Always choose lemons that feel heavy for their size: they're the ones with the most juice.

Frozen Strawberry Daiquiri

This is a spinoff version of the rum original. When the fresh fruit isn't in season, use drained, canned strawberries instead, but wash off the sugar syrup.

4 strawberries
½ measure/2 tsp lime juice
1 measure/1½ tbsp cognac
1 measure/1½ tbsp light rum
dash grenadine

Put the strawberries, lime juice and brandy in a liquidizer and process to a purée. Add the light rum, grenadine and half a glass of finely crushed ice and process once more to a smooth slush. Pour the resulting mixture into a well-chilled cocktail glass. Garnish with a strawberry and a small sprig of fresh mint.

Vanderbilt

This cocktail was created in 1912 in honour of Cornelius Vanderbilt, member of one of America's great plutocratic families. The flavour is certainly rich enough to do justice to the name.

1½ measures/6 tsp cognac
½ measure/2 tsp cherry brandy
2 dashes Angostura bitters
¼ measure/1 tsp sugar syrup

Shake all the ingredients well with ice, and strain into a cocktail glass. Garnish with a twist of lemon, and a couple of cherries on a cocktail stick.

Connoisseur's Treat

Certainly a treat for somebody, this is a very strong, all-alcohol mix, not to be taken lightly. The flavour is a heady combination of herbs, vanilla and orange.

1½ measures/6 tsp cognac
½ measure/2 tsp Grand Marnier
½ measure/2 tsp Galliano

Stir the ingredients in a pitcher with ice until thoroughly chilled, and strain into a rocks glass. Garnish with a twist of orange rind.

Bombay

A very strong and challenging mixture, this is the kind of drink that comes in handy in situations where Dutch courage is called for. Or should that be Indian courage?

1½ measures/6 tsp cognac
¾ measures/3 tsp dry vermouth
¾ measure/3 tsp sweet red vermouth
¼ measure/1 tsp Cointreau
¼ measure/1 tsp absinthe

Shake all the ingredients well with ice, and strain into a cocktail glass or champagne saucer filled with crushed ice. Do not garnish.

East India

This short and elegant drink can be served as an aperitif, as it has a pleasantly bitter note to it.

⅔ measure/1 tbsp cognac
2 dashes white curaçao
2 dashes pineapple juice
2 dashes Angostura bitters

Stir all the ingredients well with ice in a pitcher until chilled, and strain into a small tumbler or Old-Fashioned glass, half-filled with broken ice. Garnish with a twist of lime and a cherry.

Apple Sour

For those who don't fancy swallowing raw egg, this drink can be made without the egg white. Applejack or apple schnapps also work well in place of the calvados.

1 measure/1½ tbsp cognac
1 measure/1½ tbsp calvados
⅔ measure/1 tbsp lemon juice

5ml/1 tsp sugar
dash Angostura bitters
1 egg white

Shake all the ingredients well with ice, and strain into a tumbler half-filled with cracked ice. Garnish the drink with slices of red and green apple dipped in lemon juice.

Brandy Punch

This old-fashioned punch recipe might have graced the table of an elegant Victorian party. It's a chilled punch as well, which tends to be a bit more popular these days than the hot version. The recipe should serve around 12 guests.

Bartending know-how
Always ice the individual glasses rather than the punch bowl itself.

1 × 700ml/1 pint bottle of cognac
150ml/¼ pint orange curaçao
1 measure/1½ tbsp grenadine
juice of 5 lemons
juice of 2 oranges
250ml/8fl oz mineral water
orange and lemon slices
400ml/14fl oz sparkling ginger ale

Mix all but the last ingredient in a punch bowl and add the ginger ale just before serving. Ladle into highball glasses packed with ice.

Lemon Lady

This is a delightful concoction that will have guests coming back for more. It could be served between courses as a more invigorating alternative to a straight sorbet.

1 measure/1½ tbsp cognac
½ measure/2 tsp Cointreau
3 measures/4½ tbsp light, partially melted
   lemon sorbet

Shake well with ice to combine the sorbet, and strain into a chilled cocktail glass. Garnish with a slice of lemon.

Never on Sunday

This recipe uses Metaxa, the softly caramelly Greek brandy, together with its compatriot, aniseedy ouzo, for a thoroughly Mediterranean experience.

1 measure/1½ tbsp Metaxa
½ measure/2 tsp ouzo
dash lemon juice

dash Angostura bitters
2 measures/3 tbsp dry sparkling wine
2 measures/3 tbsp sparkling ginger ale

Stir the first four ingredients in a pitcher with ice, strain into a tall glass and top up with the sparkling wine and ginger ale. Garnish with a slice of lemon.

Grenadier

This drink is a brandy variation on the Whisky Mac, and equally good at cheering up those suffering with a winter chill.

1 measure/1½ tbsp cognac
1 measure/1½ tbsp green ginger wine
5ml/1 tsp caster (superfine) sugar

Shake all the ingredients well with ice, and strain into a small tumbler. Drink quickly so that the warmth of the alcohol pervades the system in a comforting way.

Cranberry Kiss

In this delicious, full-flavoured cocktail, the tang of cranberry and pink grapefruit juices is balanced by the toffeeish sweetness of marsala.

redcurrants, to garnish
1 egg white, lightly beaten, and 15ml/1 tbsp
   caster (superfine) sugar, to garnish
1 measure/1½ tbsp cognac
2 measures/3 tbsp cranberry juice
2 measures/3 tbsp pink grapefruit juice
2 measures/3 tbsp marsala dolce

For the garnish, lightly brush the redcurrants with the egg white. Shake sugar over them to cover with a frosting. Set aside to dry. Shake the brandy, and cranberry and grapefruit juices with ice and strain into a well-chilled glass. Tilt the glass slightly before slowly pouring in the marsala down the side. Garnish with the frosted redcurrants.

Hard Case

For a small drink with a sharply fruity flavour, this is something of a misnomer. It's a (relatively) harmless customer.

1½ measures/6 tsp cognac
½ measure/2 tsp crème de cassis
¼ measure/1 tsp lemon juice

Shake all the ingredients well with ice, and strain into a cocktail glass. Garnish with a half-slice of lemon.

Champarelle

Dating from the late 19th century, this is one of the oldest recipes for the layered drink known as a pousse-café. It helps if the ingredients and the glass itself are pre-chilled, as they are not mixed in any way, and you can't put ice in the drink.

½ measure/2 tsp orange curaçao
½ measure/2 tsp yellow Chartreuse

Brandy Fino

The name tells you more or less what's in this, though the splash of Glayva may sneak craftily up on you.

1½ measures/6 tsp cognac
½ measure/2 tsp pale dry (fino) sherry
¼ measure/1 tsp Glayva

Stir all the ingredients well in a pitcher with ice until the mixture is properly chilled, and strain into a balloon glass. Do not garnish.

½ measure/2 tsp anisette
½ measure/2 tsp cognac

Carefully pour each of the ingredients in this order over the back of a large spoon into a liqueur glass or sherry schooner, ensuring that they remain in separate layers. Use a clean spoon for each ingredient.

Blackjack

Perhaps invented to steady nerves at the gaming table, this mix is more likely to impair concentration. It is a stimulating one nonetheless.

1 measure/1½ tbsp cognac
½ measure/2 tsp kirsch
½ measure/2 tsp Kahlúa
2 measures/3 tbsp cold black coffee

Shake all the ingredients well with ice, and pour without straining into a rocks glass. Do not garnish.

Bartending know-how
Kirsch made in Germany tends to be drier and higher in alcohol than the versions made in the Alsace region of France. The best French grade is labelled "pur". Avoid anything labelled "Kirsch de Cuisine".

Arago

This delightful creamy creation is quite as irresistible as the Pompeii, below.

1½ measures/6 tsp cognac
1 measure/1½ tbsp crème de banane
1 measure/1½ tbsp double (heavy) cream

Shake all the ingredients well with ice, and strain into a cocktail glass. Sprinkle the surface of the drink with grated dark chocolate.

Pompeii

Here is a different spin on the Alexander formula, but with the chocolate component given a sweeter, nutty edge.

1 measure/1½ tbsp cognac
¾ measure/3 tsp white crème de cacao
½ measure/2 tsp amaretto
1 measure/1½ tbsp double (heavy) cream

Shake all the ingredients well with ice, and strain into a cocktail glass. Sprinkle the drink's surface with flaked almonds.

Last Goodbye

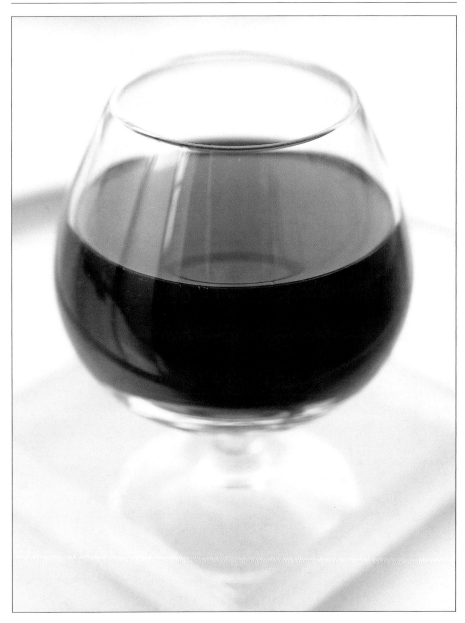

The flavours of cherry brandy and Cointreau are seen as being particularly compatible with cognac, and this is another appealing mixture.

1 measure/1½ tbsp cognac
¾ measure/3 tsp cherry brandy

¼ measure/1 tsp Cointreau
½ measure/2 tsp lime juice
¼ measure/1 tsp grenadine

Shake all the ingredients well with ice, and strain into a balloon glass. You could garnish with a lime slice and a cherry.

Incredible

Chartreuse doesn't often mix well with other spirits, but this is definitely worth a go, Incredible as it may seem.

1 measure/1½ tbsp cognac
½ measure/2 tsp green Chartreuse

½ measure/2 tsp cherry brandy

Stir all the ingredients gently with ice in a pitcher until well-chilled, and then strain into a rocks glass. Garnish with a cocktail cherry.

Missile Stopper

On a military hardware theme, this fruity little number should stop anyone in their tracks.

1 measure/1½ tbsp cognac
½ measure/2 tsp crème de fraise
1 measure/1½ tbsp grapefruit juice
1 measure/1½ tbsp pineapple juice
¼ measure/1 tsp grenadine

Shake all the ingredients well with ice, and strain into a chilled balloon glass. Garnish with a sliver of pineapple and a strawberry.

Port Side

The purply-red colour of this very sophisticated short drink looks very fetching sinking through a snowdrift of crushed ice.

1½ measures/6 tsp cognac
½ measure/2 tsp ruby port
½ measure/2 tsp crème de mûre

Stir all the ingredients with ice in a pitcher, and strain into a rocks glass half-filled with crushed ice. Garnish with a blackberry, if you happen to have one to hand.

Torpedo

I have come across a variety of different mixtures under this title. This seems to me to be the one most worthy of the name. It's very dry, spirity and strong, and its name reflects something of the force with which it will go through you.

1½ measures/6 tsp cognac
¾ measure/3 tsp calvados
dash gin

Shake all the ingredients well with ice, and strain into a pre-chilled cocktail glass. Garnish with a twist of lemon.

Coterie

Strong and sour, this is just the way a grown-up cocktail should be. Robert Cross's recipe suggests Chartreuse as an alternative to the hard-to-find, but similar, Basque liqueur, Izarra.

1 measure/1½ tbsp cognac
½ measure/2 tsp yellow Chartreuse
½ measure/2 tsp gin
¼ measure/1 tsp lemon juice
¼ measure/1 tsp sugar syrup

Stir all the ingredients well with ice in a pitcher, and strain the drink into a chilled small tumbler. Garnish with a half-slice of lemon.

Fighter

This combative mixture is rendered seemingly tamer by the sparkling top-up. Do not be deceived.

1 measure/1½ tbsp cognac
½ measure/2 tsp vodka
½ measure/2 tsp Mandarine Napoléon
4 measures/6 tbsp sparkling bitter lemon

Add the first three ingredients to a highball glass half-filled with cracked ice. Stir vigorously. Top up with the bitter lemon. Garnish with a slice of mandarin orange, clementine, satsuma or similar.

Pisco Sour

The origin of pisco, the colourless brandy of South America, is energetically disputed between Peru and Chile. This is the classic way of taking it locally.

juice of half a lime
5ml/1 tsp caster (superfine) sugar
2 measures/3 tbsp pisco

Bayou

The peachiness of this cocktail evokes the southern United States, as does its name. It's rich and fruity, with a refreshing sour finish.

1½ measures/6 tsp cognac
½ measure/2 tsp peach brandy
1 measure/1½ tbsp peach juice
⅓ measure/1½ tsp lime juice

Shake all the ingredients well with ice, and strain into a rocks glass. Garnish with a slice of ultra-ripe white peach.

Half-fill a small tumbler with smashed ice. Squeeze the lime juice directly into the glass and drop in the wrung-out shell. Add the sugar and stir well to dissolve it. Now add the pisco, and give the drink a final stir. A dash of Angostura bitters can be added too, if desired, but it isn't essential.

Apricot Bellini

This is a version of the famous aperitif served at Harry's Bar in Venice. Instead of the usual sparkling wine and peach juice, apricot nectar and apricot brandy make this a tempting, and stronger, variation. This recipe serves six to eight.

3 ripe apricots
½ measure/2 tsp lemon juice
½ measure/2 tsp sugar syrup
1 measure/1½ tbsp cognac
1 measure/1½ tbsp apricot brandy
1 bottle brut champagne or dry sparkling wine, chilled

Plunge the apricots into boiling water for 2 minutes to loosen the skins, then peel and pit them. Discard the pits and skin. Process the apricot flesh with the lemon juice until you have a smooth purée. Sweeten to taste with sugar syrup, then strain. Add the brandy and liqueur to the apricot nectar and stir together. Divide the apricot nectar among chilled champagne flutes. Finish the drinks with chilled champagne or sparkling wine.

Dizzy Dame

Well, she will be after drinking two or three of these. Another of those creamy cocktails full of rich, indulgent flavours (and calories).

1 measure/1½ tbsp cognac
¾ measure/3 tsp Tia Maria
½ measure/2 tsp cherry brandy
¾ measure/3 tsp double (heavy) cream

Shake all the ingredients well with ice, and strain into a cocktail glass. Garnish with a cherry.

Captain Kidd

Brandy and dark rum make a heady, but very successful mix in a powerful cocktail, and this one is further enhanced by the addition of strong chocolate flavour. There are no non-alcoholic ingredients, you'll notice, so watch out.

Mikado

This is a 1920s Savoy Hotel recipe of great charm. The Gilbert and Sullivan work of the same name was premiered at the Savoy Theatre in 1885.

1½ measures/6 tsp cognac
2 dashes orange curaçao
2 dashes crème de noyau
2 dashes orgeat syrup (or amaretto)
2 dashes Angostura bitters

Shake all the ingredients well with ice, and strain into a cocktail glass. Garnish with a half-slice of orange and a cherry.

1½ measures/6 tsp cognac
1 measure/1½ tbsp dark rum
1 measure/1½ tbsp brown crème de cacao

Shake well with ice, and strain into a chilled champagne saucer. Garnish with a physalis or a half-slice of orange.

Savoy Hotel

It's a short step from London's Savoy Theatre to the American Bar in the hotel itself, where this delightful cocktail (like many another) was created. It's a pousse-café or layered drink that requires a steady hand.

1 measure/1½ tbsp brown crème de cacao
1 measure/1½ tbsp Bénédictine
1 measure/1½ tbsp cognac

Carefully pour each of the ingredients, in this order, over the back of a spoon into a liqueur glass or sherry schooner to create a multi-layered drink. Serve immediately, while the effect is intact.

Harvard

This mixture was invented at the distinguished Ivy League university in the 1920s. It originally had equal quantities of brandy and vermouth and no lemon juice, but this is a less sweet and altogether more balanced mixture.

1½ measures/6 tsp cognac
½ measure/2 tsp sweet red vermouth
¼ measure/1 tsp lemon juice
¼ measure/1 tsp grenadine
2 dashes Angostura bitters

Shake all the ingredients well with ice, and strain into a cocktail glass. Garnish with a twist of lemon.

Brandy Melba

As might be expected, this is a very fruity cocktail that could almost pass as a sort of dessert. It uses the combination of peach and raspberry in the classic Peach Melba dessert.

1½ measures/6 tsp cognac
½ measure/2 tsp peach schnapps
¼ measure/1 tsp crème de framboise
½ measure/2 tsp lemon juice
¼ measure/1 tsp orange bitters (or curaçao)

Shake well with ice, and strain into a chilled cocktail glass. Garnish with a slice of ripe peach and a raspberry.

Lake Como

The geographical reference recalls the origins of the excellent Italian liqueur used in this recipe. You'll never want another Black Russian after tasting this.

1½ measures/6 tsp cognac
¾ measure/3 tsp Tuaca

Mix the ingredients well with ice in a large glass, and strain into an Old-Fashioned or small rocks glass. Squeeze a twist of lemon rind over the drink and then drop it into the glass. This is one for drinking quickly and confidently.

Fjord

Good Scandinavian aquavit is needed for this recipe. The name suggests Norwegian, but Swedish or Danish would do quite as well.

1 measure/1½ tbsp cognac
½ measure/2 tsp aquavit
1 measure/1½ tbsp orange juice

½ measure/2 tsp lime juice
¼ measure/1 tsp grenadine

Shake all the ingredients well with ice, and strain into a chilled rocks glass half-filled with cracked ice. Garnish the drink with half-slices of orange and lime.

Booster

This egg-white drink has a powerful kick. You may find it helps to whisk the egg white for a few seconds before adding it to the shaker, just to ensure the right kind of foamy texture in the finished drink.

2 measures/3 tbsp cognac
1 measure/1½ tbsp orange curaçao
½ egg white

Shake all the ingredients very thoroughly with ice, and strain into a cocktail glass. Sprinkle the surface with ground nutmeg.

Via Veneto

Named after the street in Rome that was once a scene of bohemian glamour, this cocktail contains the Italian elderberry-flavoured liqueur Sambuca Romana.

1½ measures/6 tsp cognac
½ measure/2 tsp Sambuca
½ measure/2 tsp lemon juice
¼ measure/1 tsp sugar syrup
½ egg white

Shake all the ingredients well with ice, and strain into a chilled rocks glass. Garnish with a slice of lemon.

Memphis Belle

One of the earliest cocktail recipes to use Southern Comfort, this may look an unlikely idea, in that it blends a whiskey-based liqueur with brandy, but in its dry, sharply sour way, it works.

1½ measures/6 tsp cognac
¾ measure/3 tsp Southern Comfort
½ measure/2 tsp lemon juice
¼ measure/1 tsp orange bitters (or curaçao)

Shake all the ingredients well with ice, and strain into a pre-chilled cocktail glass. Garnish with a twist of lemon.

Kiss the Boys Goodbye

As the name suggests, this is a cocktail with which American troops going off to serve in the Second World War were toasted. It seemed to do the trick.

1 measure/1½ tbsp cognac
1 measure/1½ tbsp sloe gin
¼ measure/1 tsp lemon juice
½ egg white

Shake all the ingredients well with ice, and strain into a rocks glass half-filled with cracked ice. Garnish with a wedge of lemon.

Coffee Cognac Cooler

This drink is unabashedly decadent, and not for those counting calories. The recipe serves two, so you can both feel guilty together.

250ml/8fl oz cold strong dark-roast coffee
80ml/3fl oz cognac
50ml/2fl oz coffee liqueur
50ml/2fl oz double (heavy) cream
10ml/2 tsp sugar
2 scoops coffee ice cream

Shake or blend all the ingredients except the ice cream, together with plenty of crushed ice. Pour into tall glasses and gently add a scoop of ice cream to each. Garnish with chocolate shavings, and serve with a long-handled spoon.

Coffee and Chocolate Flip

Use only the freshest egg in this recipe, as it isn't cooked. You could replace the Kahlúa with Tia Maria for a slightly sweeter version. The result is a smoothly frothy, intensely rich drink with a strong, beguiling coffee flavour. The chocolate element is confined to the garnish.

1 egg
5ml/1 tsp sugar
1 measure/1½ tbsp cognac
1 measure/1½ tbsp Kahlúa
5ml/1 tsp dark-roast instant coffee granules
3 measures/4½ tbsp double (heavy) cream

Separate the egg and lightly beat the white until frothy. In a separate bowl, beat the egg yolk with the sugar. In a small pan, combine the brandy, Kahlúa,

coffee and cream and warm over a very low heat. Allow the mixture to cool, then whisk it into the egg yolk. Add the egg white to the egg and cream, and pour the mixture briefly back and forth between two glasses until it is smooth. Pour into a tall glass over coarsely crushed ice and sprinkle the top with cocoa powder.

Café Royale

This is a highly sophisticated, and rather ostentatious digestif. The recipe serves four.

4 sugar cubes
300ml/½ pint hot, strong, black filter or cafetière coffee
4 measures/6 tbsp cognac

Rinse out four coffee cups with boiled water and pour away. Add a sugar lump to each cup and then fill with coffee to a little way below the rim. Float a measure of cognac on the surface, and then set it alight. Guests should allow the drink to flame for a few seconds, and then extinguish it by stirring with a spoon.

Alhambra Royale

We conclude our brandy repertoire with a hot chocolate mixture that tastes even more luxurious than the preceding coffee recipes.

hot chocolate, made up to just short of the cup's brim
1 small piece orange rind
1½ measures/6 tsp cognac
15ml/1 tbsp whipped cream

Drop the orange rind into the hot chocolate. Heat the cognac in a metal ladle over a gas flame or over boiling water, and set it alight. Pour it, flaming, into the chocolate. Stir it in, and spoon a blob of whipped cream on to the surface of the drink. Sprinkle with cocoa powder.

Bartending know-how

When using hot chocolate in a cocktail, it is always preferable to use proper cocoa with a good, high proportion of real cacao solids in it. The alternative – drinking chocolate – is mostly sugar and has a much less concentrated flavour.

Other spirits

In this section, we deal with those less well-known spirits that fall outside the main six. These will include the bitter aperitifs, such as Campari, as well as the concentrated bitters like Angostura; the apple brandies, such as France's calvados and America's applejack; and the traditional European fruit distillates, such as kirsch (made from cherries) and slivovitz (plums). Despite their minority status, these products have played an integral part in the cocktail repertoire, and will no doubt continue to do so.

Americano

A recipe going back to the early years of the 20th century, Americano was the one of the first to make a feature of the bitter red Italian *aperitivo*, Campari.

2 measures/3 tbsp sweet red vermouth
1 measure/1½ tbsp Campari
1 measure/1½ tbsp soda water

Add the first two ingredients to a rocks glass or Old-Fashioned glass with two or three cubes of ice in it. Stir, and add the soda. Squeeze a twist of orange rind over the drink and then drop it in.

Negroni

The Negroni is an Americano with gin, making an altogether drier drink. It is named after one Count Negroni who invented this formula at a bar in Florence just after the First World War. The addition of gin elevates the drink into a different class altogether. This is a brilliant aperitif.

2 measures/3 tbsp gin
1 measure/1½ tbsp sweet red vermouth
¾ measure/3 tsp Campari
1 measure/1½ tbsp soda water

Mix the first three ingredients in a tumbler with ice and then add the soda. Finish with orange, as for Americano.

Pink Gin

The famous tipple of British naval officers (the lower ranks drank rum), this is simply a neat, bittered gin. Classically, it should be made with Plymouth gin, for its milder aromatic quality and its naval associations.

Sprinkle about six drops of Angostura bitters into a goblet-shaped glass, roll it around to coat the inner surfaces, then dash it out. Add ice-cold gin, which will then take on the faintest pink tint.

Normandy Cooler

This refreshing summer drink is perfect for afternoons in the garden. It can be made with applejack instead of calvados and renamed a Harvard Cooler, in which it is as well to leave out the grenadine.

2 measures/3 tbsp calvados
1 measure/1½ tbsp lemon juice
¼ measure/1 tsp grenadine
½ measure/2 tsp sugar syrup
4 measures/6 tbsp soda water

Fill a highball glass with cracked ice and dangle a twist of lemon in it. Add the first four ingredients, give the drink a good stir, and then top up with the soda water.

Calvados Cream

The cheaper grades of calvados can be a little fiery. If that's what you have to hand, this should sort it out. It's a creamy, but sharply flavoured cocktail.

2 measures/3 tbsp calvados
½ measure/2 tsp lemon juice

1 measure/1½ tbsp double (heavy) cream
¼ measure/1 tsp pineapple syrup (from a can)

Shake the first three ingredients thoroughly with ice, and strain into a bowl-shaped cocktail glass. Sprinkle the pineapple syrup over the surface.

Depth Charge

This is one of several 1920s cocktails that owe their names to the World War then still fresh in everyone's memory.

1 measure/1½ tbsp calvados
1 measure/1½ tbsp cognac

½ measure/2 tsp lemon juice
¼ measure/1 tsp grenadine

Shake all the ingredients well with ice, and strain into a cocktail glass. Garnish with a twist of lemon.

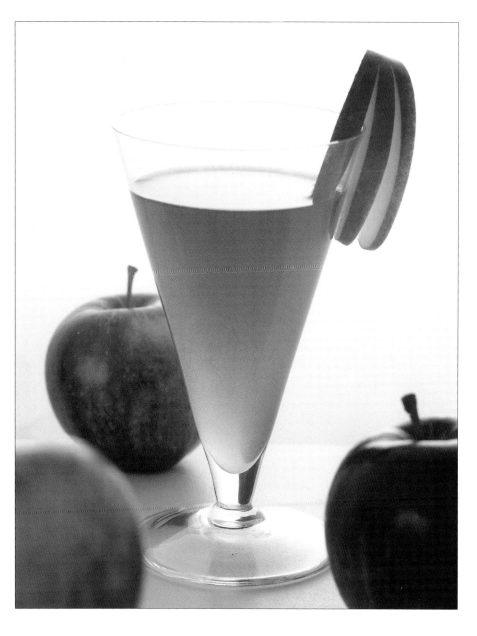

Calvarniac

The name of this drink is a combination of its three alcoholic ingredients. It is an impeccably French mixture, and a very fine one.

1 measure/1½ tbsp calvados
⅔ measure/1 tbsp Grand Marnier
⅓ measure/1½ tsp cognac
1 measure/1½ tbsp sparkling lemonade

Half-fill a rocks glass with cracked ice, and add the first three ingredients. Stir briskly, and then add the lemonade. Garnish with a slice of lemon.

French Toddy

This is a variation of a very old French recipe, said to have been a favourite of the novelist Gustave Flaubert, to which coffee and sugar have been added. This recipe serves two.

120ml/4fl oz calvados
50ml/2fl oz apricot brandy
20–30ml/4–6 tsp sugar, to taste
300ml/½ pint very strong coffee (filter/
    cafetière brewed at about 45g/8 tbsp
    coffee per 500ml/17fl oz water)

Applecart

This is another American recipe, but one that can just as easily be made with calvados as with applejack – or with home-grown Somerset cider brandy, for that matter.

1 measure/1½ tbsp applejack
¾ measure/3 tsp Cointreau
½ measure/2 tsp lemon juice

Shake all the ingredients well with ice, and strain into a chilled cocktail glass. Garnish the drink with a half-slice of lemon.

25ml/1½ tbsp double (heavy) cream

Very gently warm the calvados and apricot brandy together over a low heat, and transfer to large balloon glasses. Dissolve the sugar in the coffee and add to the liquor. Stir vigorously. While the contents are still rotating from the stirring, pour the cream over the surface in a circular motion. Do not stir further, just sip and savour.

Apple Blossom

The slightly sweeter finish of applejack is better suited than calvados in this American cocktail. Use ordinary sugar syrup if you can't get hold of maple, although it won't be quite the same.

1½ measures/6 tsp applejack
1 measure/1½ tbsp apple juice
½ measure/2 tsp lemon juice
¼ measure/1 tsp maple syrup

Shake all the ingredients well with ice, and strain into a cocktail glass or champagne saucer. Garnish with a wafer-thin slice of red apple with the skin left on, and a half-slice of lemon.

Bartending know-how
Applejack was the accidental product of early American settlers. It was only when the hops they tried to make beer with failed that they turned to apples instead.

Rose

Although it looks delicately pink and sweet, the cocktail that this 1920s recipe actually produces is very dry, and would make a good aperitif.

1 measure/1½ tbsp kirsch
1½ measures/6 tsp dry vermouth
dash grenadine

Shake all the ingredients well with ice, and strain into a cocktail glass. You could garnish the drink with a cherry.

Bartending know-how
Kirsch and cherry brandy are not interchangeable, since the former is drier than the latter, and colourless. Cherry brandy is also lower in alcohol.

Vruiça Rakia

This is how slivovitz, the Balkan plum spirit, is often drunk in its regions of origin. It is a cold-weather preparation intended to insulate the outdoor worker. This recipe serves two.

4 measures/6 tbsp slivovitz
10ml/2 tsp soft brown sugar

Pit Stop

If Rose is too dry for you, this fizzy, fruity kirsch cocktail is definitely a more sweet-natured proposition.

1 measure/1½ tbsp kirsch
1 measure/1½ tbsp cherry brandy
¼ measure/1 tsp amaretto
2 measures/3 tbsp sparkling lemonade

Half-fill a rocks glass with cracked ice. Add the first three ingredients, stir and add the lemonade. Garnish with a twist of lemon and a couple of cherries on a cocktail stick.

4 measures/6 tbsp water

Put all the ingredients in a small pan and bring nearly to the boil, stirring to dissolve the sugar. Pour into mugs or heatproof glasses, and garnish with blueberries skewered on to a swizzle-stick. Drink while hot.

Slivovitz Fizz

A refreshing, cold, sparkling cocktail to complement the hot slivovitz above, this makes a original alternative to more mainstream long drinks.

2 measures/3 tbsp slivovitz
½ measure/2 tsp lime juice
¼ measure/1 tsp sugar syrup
4 measures/6 tbsp soda water

Shake the first three ingredients well with ice, and strain into a highball glass, half-filled with cracked ice. Top up with soda. Garnish with a slice of black plum.

Liqueurs

The world of cocktails would be virtually nothing without liqueurs. They are what give character and personality to many recipes. Sometimes they can be relied on to add sweetness as well as flavour to a drink, so that no other sugaring agent is needed, and sometimes – as in the case of the old herbal liqueurs like Chartreuse, Bénédictine and Strega – they add their peculiar aromatic quality to basic spirits. New liqueurs are being produced and included all the time (Malibu and Midori became firm cocktail flavourites in the 1980s), and, among the recipes that follow, you will find at least one or two appearances of nearly all the liqueurs discussed earlier.

Sidecar

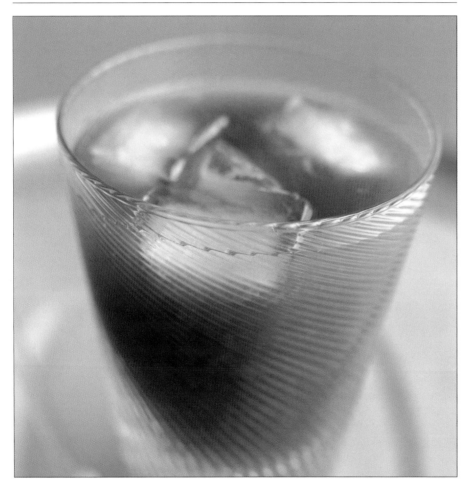

Cointreau can successfully be mixed with virtually any spirit (except perhaps whisky) and a quantity of lemon juice, and shaken with ice. Start with gin and you have a White Lady, vodka for a Balalaika and even tequila for a lemon Margarita. The brandy version in a Paris classic called Sidecar, after the preferred means of travel of a French army officer.

1½ measures/6 tsp cognac
¾ measure/3 tsp Cointreau
¾ measure/3 tsp lemon juice

Shake well with ice and strain into a rocks glass with a little cracked ice. Garnish with a half-slice of lemon.

Rum Sidecar

Just to complete the Sidecar repertoire, here's a version of the basic mix that uses light or golden rum. It produces a very slightly sweeter final result.

1½ measures/6 tsp light rum
¾ measure/3 tsp Cointreau
¾ measure/3 tsp lemon juice

Shake all the ingredients well with ice, and strain into a cocktail glass. Garnish with a half-slice of lemon.

Between the Sheets

A 1920s recipe that suddenly became very fashionable again in the 1980s, this is a powerful, sharply flavoured cocktail. Some recipes use light rum instead of white, but the resulting colour is inevitably slightly muddier.

1 measure/1½ tbsp Cointreau
1 measure/1½ tbsp cognac
1 measure/1½ tbsp white rum
½ measure/2 tsp lemon juice

Shake all the ingredients well with ice, and strain into a bowl-shaped cocktail glass. Garnish with a twist of lemon.

Bartending know-how
The principal flavouring element in crème de menthe – green or white – is peppermint. Its flavour is more subtly aromatic and refreshing than that of spearmint.

Stinger

The adaptable Stinger is simply a two-thirds-one-third mixture of any spirit with white crème de menthe, shaken with ice and served over smashed ice in a cocktail glass. The prototype version, dating from around the time of the First World War, is with cognac, as in the following recipe.

2 measures/3 tbsp cognac
1 measure/1½ tbsp white crème de menthe

Shake both the ingredients well with ice, and strain into a cocktail glass. You could garnish it with a tuft of mint, although it is fine without.

Grasshopper

This is a minted, creamy cocktail in an attractive shade of green. If you use dark crème de cacao, the cocktail will not be as vibrant a colour, but you'll find that it tastes just as good.

1 measure/1½ tbsp green crème de menthe
1 measure/1½ tbsp white crème de cacao
1 measure/1½ tbsp double (heavy) cream

Charlie Chaplin

The first, and in many ways the greatest, cocktail era was also the age of silent films, and it is no surprise to hear that, just as Mary Pickford was honoured with a cocktail named after her, so was the greatest silent comic of them all.

1½ measures/6 tsp sloe gin
½ measure/2 tsp apricot brandy
½ measure/2 tsp lime juice

Shake all the ingredients well with ice, and strain into a chilled cocktail glass. Garnish with a slice of lime, and perhaps a sliver of apricot.

Shake all the ingredients very well with ice, and strain into a cocktail glass. Sprinkle the surface with grated chocolate. Alternatively, decorate with chocolate curls, made by pouring melted chocolate on to a cold baking tray, allowing to harden and then scraping gently off with the point of a knife.

Snowball

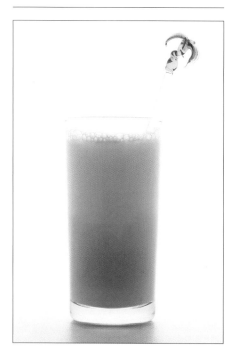

This is the kind of cocktail generally considered safe to give to minors, since it resembles nothing so much as a particularly rich milkshake. It is almost the only thing worth doing with advocaat. If you require a bit more of a kick, add ½ measure/2 tsp sweet brown cream sherry as well.

2 measures/3 tbsp advocaat
5 measures/120ml/4fl oz ice-cold sparkling
   lemonade

Add to a highball glass half-filled with cracked ice, and stir gently. You could garnish with a cherry on a stick.

Bartending know-how
Snowball needs plenty of lemonade to avoid its texture being too cloying.

Hollywood Nuts

Almond and hazelnut are among the flavours in this cocktail. The original recipe has egg white in it too, but I don't tend to feel it needs it.

1 measure/1½ tbsp white rum
½ measure/2 tsp amaretto
½ measure/2 tsp brown crème de cacao
½ measure/2 tsp Frangelico
1 measure/1½ tbsp sparkling lemonade

Shake all but the last ingredient with ice, and strain into a rocks glass half-filled with cracked ice. Add the lemonade and stir. Garnish with a slice of lemon.

B52

This cocktail depends on the difference in specific weight or densities of each of the liqueurs to remain separated.

1 measure/1½ tbsp Kahlúa
1 measure/1½ tbsp Bailey's Irish Cream
1 measure/1½ tbsp Grand Marnier

Round the World

This cocktail certainly contains a cosmopolitan mix of ingredients. I can think of no other obvious explanation for its name.

1½ measure/6 tsp green crème de menthe
1 measure/1½ tbsp gin
2½ measures/3½ tbsp pineapple juice

Shake all the ingredients well with ice, and strain into a chilled wine goblet. Garnish with a chunk of pineapple on a cocktail stick.

Pour the ingredients in this order over the back of a cold teaspoon into a shot glass or liqueur glass, remembering to change the spoon between shots. If you can't get the hang of the layering, just shake it all up with ice and strain it into a cocktail glass.

Hooded Claw

Syrupy-sweet prune juice with amaretto and Cointreau makes a delicious digestif when poured over a snow of finely crushed ice. If you can't get it, you could try using the liquor from a can of prunes, although It may well be composed of other fruit juices. This recipe serves four people.

5 measures/120ml/4fl oz prune juice
2 measures/3 tbsp amaretto
1 measure/1½ tbsp Cointreau

Shake all the ingredients well with ice, and strain into four small liqueur glasses loosely filled with crushed ice.

Shamrock

Best described as something of an acquired taste, your view of this drink will depend crucially on how well you get on with the combination of green Chartreuse and mint. The Irish theme accounts for all the greenery. And it is, of course, an incredibly strong alcoholic drink.

1 measure/1½ tbsp Irish whiskey
1 measure/1½ tbsp dry vermouth
¼ measure/1 tsp green Chartreuse
¼ measure/1 tsp green crème de menthe

Stir all the ingredients well with ice in a pitcher, and strain into a cocktail glass. Garnish with a green olive.

Airstrike

This is a burning drink, similar to the Italian flaming Sambuca tradition.

2 measures/3 tbsp Galliano
1 measure/1½ tbsp cognac
1 star anise

Heat the Galliano and brandy in a small pan until just warm. Pour into a heat-resistant glass and add the star anise. Using a long match, pass the flame over the surface of the drink to ignite it, being careful not to burn yourself. Let it burn for a couple of minutes, until the star anise has begun to sizzle a little and released its aroma into the drink. Leave to cool slightly before drinking.

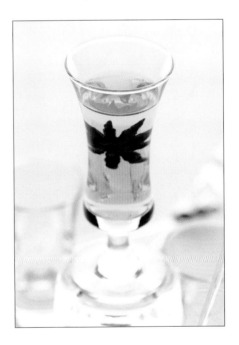

Bullfrog

This is a very simple mix for apricot brandy, in which the generous quantity of lemon juice takes all the sweetness off the liqueur.

1½ measures/6 tsp apricot brandy
juice of a lemon

Shake both the ingredients well with ice and strain into a cocktail glass. Garnish with a slice of lemon.

Long Island Iced Tea

Las Hadas

This contemporary classic spin on the traditional Sambuca presentation is for those who aren't quite up to tackling a drink that's been set on fire.

1 measure/1½ tbsp Sambuca
1 measure/1½ tbsp Kahlúa

Stir both ingredients well with ice in a mixing glass, and strain into a pre-chilled wine goblet. Float a few coffee beans on the surface of the drink.

Alaska

This drink is intended to evoke the frozen wastes, so make sure it's shaken until the cocktail shaker is almost too cold to hold.

1½ measures/6 tsp gin
½ measure/2 tsp yellow Chartreuse

Shake both the ingredients very well with plenty of ice, and strain into a cocktail glass. No garnish is necessary.

This is a long, powerful drink with a rumbustiously intoxicating effect, its potency well disguised by the cola. For a simpler version, use equal quantities of rum, Cointreau, tequila and lemon juice, and top up with cola. The recipe does not contain tea. It's a facetious way of referring to the fact that it looks innocuously like a glass of non-alcoholic iced tea.

½ measure/2 tsp white rum
½ measure/2 tsp vodka

½ measure/2 tsp gin
½ measure/2 tsp silver tequila
½ measure/2 tsp Cointreau
juice of half a lemon
½ measure/2 tsp sugar syrup
4 measures/6 tbsp cola

Stir all but the last ingredient well with ice for about 30 seconds in a pitcher to chill. Strain into a highball glass filled with ice cubes and a twist of lemon. Add chilled cola, and finish with a sprig of fresh mint.

Old William

This is a gorgeously fruity mixture that brings out the best in the delightful liqueur Poire William. The citrus juices take the edge off its sweetness.

2 measures/3 tbsp Poire William
½ measure/2 tsp maraschino

½ measure/2 tsp orange juice
½ measure/2 tsp lemon juice

Add the ingredients in this order to a rocks glass half-filled with broken ice. Stir briskly, and garnish with half-slices of orange and lemon.

Bijou

This recipe dates from the 1920s. The mix of Chartreuse and vermouth does indeed create a rather jewel-like colour. It must be Plymouth gin, by the way.

1 measure/1½ tbsp Plymouth gin
1 measure/1½ tbsp green Chartreuse
1 measure/1½ tbsp sweet red vermouth
dash orange bitters (or curaçao)

Stir all the ingredients well with ice in a pitcher, and then strain into a cocktail glass. Squeeze a twist of lemon over the drink, drop it in and add a cherry.

Frosty Amour

This drink would make a good tipple for a Valentine's Day evening in. Any frostiness will soon be dispelled after downing one.

1 measure/1½ tbsp vodka
1 measure/1½ tbsp apricot brandy
1 measure/1½ tbsp Southern Comfort
¼ measure/1 tsp Parfait Amour
¼ measure/1 tsp crème de banane
4 measures/6 tbsp 7-Up

Frost the rim of a highball glass with lemon juice and caster (superfine) sugar. Half-fill it with ice. Shake all but the last ingredient with ice, and strain into the prepared glass. Top with 7-Up. Garnish with a cherry and a slice of orange.

Fuzzy Navel

The evocative name of this drink plays on the ideas of the fuzzy-skinned peach and the navel orange. If it tastes a little too tame, add a measure of vodka to it and call it a Hairy Navel, a grown-up version of the same body part.

2 measures/3 tbsp peach schnapps
4 measures/6 tbsp orange juice

Add the ingredients to a highball glass half-filled with cracked ice, and stir well. Garnish with a slice of orange.

Singapore Sling

One of the all-time greats, Singapore Sling was created in 1915 at the world-famous Raffles Hotel in Singapore. Some recipes omit the soda for a slightly stronger drink. Some add a dash of grenadine just to deepen the pink colour, but it should nonetheless be no more than a fairly delicate blush.

2 measures/3 tbsp gin
⅔ measure/1 tbsp cherry brandy
⅔ measure/1 tbsp Cointreau
juice of 1 lemon
5ml/1 tsp caster (superfine) sugar
3 measures/4½ tbsp soda water

Shake all but the last ingredient well with ice, and strain into a highball glass. Add the soda, and decorate with a twist of lemon and a black cherry pierced with two cocktail sticks.

Zam

This is a very resourceful cocktail that uses no fewer than three liqueurs, without the need for a plain spirit base. This enhances the herbal flavours well, and the overall effect is nicely balanced between sweet and dry.

1 measure/1½ tbsp Glayva
½ measure/2 tsp Bénédictine
½ measure/2 tsp Sambuca
1½ measures/6 tsp orange juice
¼ measure/1 tsp sugar syrup
¼ measure/1 tsp lemon juice

Shake all the ingredients well with ice, and strain into a chilled champagne saucer or wine goblet loaded with crushed ice. Garnish with a strawberry.

Blanche

Another three-way liqueur blend, this one is fairly sweet, although the curaçao adds a balancing bitter note. To live up to its name, the curaçao really ought to be the white variety, but nobody will know if you use orange.

1 measure/1½ tbsp Cointreau
1 measure/1½ tbsp white curaçao
1 measure/1½ tbsp anisette

Shake all the ingredients well with ice, and strain into a cocktail glass. Emphasize the drink's purity of colour by refraining from any garnish.

Godfather

Like the Godmother, this drink uses amaretto, but substitutes Scotch for the vodka. This makes for a more complex flavour, and the drink would make a good aperitif.

Godmother

Another very simple mixture, this is a formula to throw the sweetness of almond liqueur into relief for the more savoury-toothed. It should properly be made with the most famous brand of amaretto, Disaronno Originale, but won't come to any harm if you use another.

1½ measures/6 tsp amaretto
1½ measures/6 tsp vodka

Mix both ingredients well in a tumbler full of cracked ice. The drink does not need any garnish.

1½ measures/6 tsp amaretto
1½ measures/6 tsp Scotch

Mix both ingredients well in a tumbler full of cracked ice. Do not garnish.

Bunny Hug

This one is not for the novice cocktail drinker as it consists only of strong alcohol, and the flavour is very dry.

1 measure/1½ tbsp gin
1 measure/1½ tbsp Scotch
1 measure/1½ tbsp Pernod

Bartending know-how
Pernod and other forms of pastis will give an instant natural cloudiness to any mixture.

Shake all the ingredients well with ice, and strain into a pre-chilled cocktail glass. The drink can be garnished with a twist of lemon.

Festival

Strictly for the sweet and creamy brigade, this is the sort of drink that might well kick off a hen night, assuming the girls need any further egging on.

1 measure/1½ tbsp apricot brandy
¾ measure/3 tsp white crème de cacao
¼ measure/1 tsp grenadine
½ measure/2 tsp double (heavy) cream

Shake all the ingredients well with ice, and strain into a chilled cocktail glass. Garnish with a cherry or two speared on a cocktail stick.

Lost Bikini

The name seems to evoke memories of Ursula Andress emerging from the waves in the first James Bond movie, or is that just wishful thinking?

¾ measure/3 tsp Galliano
¾ measure/3 tsp amaretto
½ measure/2 tsp white rum
½ measure/2 tsp lime juice
2 measures/3 tbsp unsweetened mandarin juice (from a can)

Shake all the ingredients well with ice, and strain into a champagne saucer or cocktail glass. Garnish with a half-slice of orange and a cherry.

Kir

This world-famous gastronomic aperitif was created in Burgundy, and was originally named after a mayor of Dijon. It consists of a glass of light, dry, acidic white wine with a shot of crème de cassis stirred into it (¼–½ measure/ 1–2 tsp, depending on taste). The classic wine to use is a Bourgogne Aligoté of the most recent vintage, but any fairly neutral-tasting white wine will do, so long as it is sharp with acidity.

Add the cassis to a glass of non-vintage brut champagne and the drink becomes a Kir Royale.

Stratosphere

A few drops of crème de violette are added to a glass of champagne until a mauve colour is obtained. The scentedness is then enhanced by adding a whole clove to the glass.

Oracabessa

A recipe that will use your garnishing skills to the full. The more fruit it has piled on to it, the better, but the banana slices are essential.

1 measure/1½ tbsp dark rum
1 measure/1½ tbsp crème de banane
juice of half a lemon
thin banana slices
4 measures/6 tbsp sparkling lemonade

Shake the first three ingredients well with ice, and strain into a large cocktail goblet. Float some banana on the surface of the drink, and top it up with the lemonade. Garnish lavishly with fruits.

An American violet liqueur, Crème Yvette, was at one time the only correct product to use in this very ladylike aperitif. Parfait Amour might also do.

Blackout

The name of this cocktail does not mean it necessarily induces the said state, but is more of a description of the resulting colour of the drink. It is a very harmonious and appealing cocktail mixture.

1¾ measures/2½ tbsp gin
¾ measure/3 tsp crème de mûre
juice of half a lime

Shake all the ingredients well with ice, and strain into a cocktail glass. Garnish with a slice of lime and a couple of ripe blackberries threaded carefully on to a cocktail stick.

Silver Jubilee

This was created for Queen Elizabeth's Silver Jubilee in 1977. There is a tendency now to up the gin quotient to as much as double this quantity, but I find that these proportions work perfectly well.

1 measure/1½ tbsp gin
1 measure/1½ tbsp crème de banane
1 measure/1½ tbsp double (heavy) cream

Shake all the ingredients thoroughly with ice to amalgamate the cream, and strain into a chilled cocktail glass. Grate a little dark chocolate over the surface, if desired.

Bartending know-how
Cream cocktails should generally be made with double cream, as the single version tends to be too runny.

Oasis

Blue cocktails suddenly became all the rage during the cocktail boom of the 1980s. This is a particularly satisfying mixture that's not too sweet.

2 measures/3 tbsp gin
½ measure/2 tsp blue curaçao
4 measures/6 tbsp tonic water

Pour the gin into a highball glass half-filled with cracked ice. Add the curaçao, top up with the tonic and stir gently. Garnish with a slice of lemon and a sprig of mint

English Rose

If you can find crème de roses, snap it up and use it in this very fetching cocktail that would make a fine Mother's Day toast. (Before you crack open the pink champagne, that is.)

1½ measures/6 tsp gin
¾ measure/3 tsp crème de roses
½ measure/2 tsp lemon juice
2.5ml/½ tsp caster (superfine) sugar
½ egg white

Shake all the ingredients thoroughly with ice, and strain into a wine glass. Alternatively, you can make this in the blender for that extra frothiness.

Olympic

Created for the 1924 Olympic Games in Paris, this is a gold medal-winning recipe.

1 measure/1½ tbsp cognac
1 measure/1½ tbsp orange curaçao

Whip

This lethally violent 1920s cocktail contains a lot of strong alcohol and no mixers. Caution is advised. One should be more than enough.

1 measure/1½ tbsp cognac
½ measure/2 tsp dry vermouth

1 measure/1½ tbsp orange juice

Shake all the ingredients well with ice, and strain into a cocktail glass. Garnish with a twist of orange rind.

½ measure/2 tsp sweet red vermouth
¼ measure/1 tsp orange curaçao
dash absinthe

Shake all the ingredients well with plenty of ice, and strain into a cocktail glass. You could garnish with a lemon twist.

Golden Tang

This recipe can be prepared short or long, depending on how the fancy takes you. If you serve it short, as here, use a wine glass. If you serve it long, increase the amount of orange juice to 4 measures/6 tbsp and serve it in a highball glass. The resulting drink is obviously more innocuous, but is an equally appealing aperitif long drink.

2 measures/3 tbsp vodka
1 measure/1½ tbsp Strega
½ measure/2 tsp crème de banane
½ measure/2 tsp orange juice

Shake all the ingredients well with ice, and strain into a large wine glass. Garnish with a twist of kumquat.

Golden Slipper

A group of "Golden" recipes continues with this American novelty drink from before the Second World War. I confess I haven't tried it; I suspect it may look rather prettier than it tastes.

1 measure/1½ tbsp yellow Chartreuse
1 egg yolk
1 measure/1½ tbsp Goldwasser

Pour the yellow Chartreuse into a copita or sherry glass. Drop the egg yolk whole on to the surface, and then carefully pour the Goldwasser on top.

Golden Start

An ingenious mix of Galliano, fruit juices and coconut. It also works if the curaçao is replaced with white crème de cacao.

2 measures/3 tbsp Galliano
1 measure/1½ tbsp orange juice
1 measure/1½ tbsp pineapple juice
1 measure/1½ tbsp white or orange curaçao
1 measure/1½ tbsp coconut cream

Golden Dream

This fancifully named cocktail was created by the Galliano company itself in the 1960s. It's a sweetly delicious, creamy concoction.

1 measure/1½ tbsp Galliano
1 measure/1½ tbsp Cointreau
1 measure/1½ tbsp orange juice
1 measure/1½ tbsp whipping cream

Shake all the ingredients well with ice, and strain into a bowl-shaped cocktail glass. Decorate the surface with grated orange rind.

Process the Galliano, fruit juices and curaçao in a blender. Add the cream of coconut with 15ml/1 tbsp finely crushed ice, and process until smooth and frothy. Frost the rim of the cocktail glass by dipping it into pineapple juice and caster (superfine) sugar. Pour the cocktail into the prepared glass while still frothy.

Gloom Chaser

There was once a gin cocktail called Gloom Raiser, on account of the depressant qualities that spirit was mythically supposed to have. This, presumably, was intended as the antidote to it. I think we can safely say it works. Certainly, a couple of them will probably manage to dispel (temporarily) whatever it was that was bothering you.

1 measure/1½ tbsp Grand Marnier
1 measure/1½ tbsp orange curaçao
½ measure/2 tsp lemon juice
¼ measure/1 tsp grenadine

Shake all the ingredients well with ice, and strain into a chilled cocktail glass. Garnish the drink with a single slice of orange.

Paradise

A winning 1920s formula that should certainly waft you somewhere in the direction of paradise, however fleetingly.

1½ measures/6 tsp gin
¾ measure/3 tsp apricot brandy
¾ measure/3 tsp orange juice
dash lemon juice

Shake all the ingredients well with ice, and strain into a flared wine glass. Garnish with a slices of orange, lemon and lime.

Alexander the Great

Another variation on the chocolate/coffee/cream combination, and distantly related to the classic Alexander, this drink is reputed to have been invented by the late Hollywood singing star Nelson Eddy. Indeed, in some quarters, he may well be more respectfully remembered for this recipe than for his films.

1½ measure/6 tsp vodka
½ measure/2 tsp Kahlúa
½ measure/2 tsp brown crème de cacao
½ measure/2 tsp double (heavy) cream

Tovarich

There are not many cocktail recipes with caraway-flavoured kümmel in them, but this one works very well, in its tartly bracing way.

1½ measures/6 tsp vodka
1 measure/1½ tbsp kümmel
juice of half a lime

Shake all the ingredients well with ice, and strain into a cocktail glass. Garnish the drink with a couple of rings of thinly sliced lime.

Shake all the ingredients well with plenty of ice, and strain into a cocktail glass. Add a couple of chocolate-coated coffee beans to the drink.

Bartending know-how
The liqueur components in Alexander the Great are Kahlúa and the brown version of chocolate liqueur. If your guests are sweeter-natured than this, substitute Tia Maria and white crème de cacao.

Batida Banana

A recipe created specifically for the Brazilian coconut liqueur, Batida de Coco, this is dangerously moreish, and is effectively little more than a grown-up milkshake, but none the worse for that. The fact that it uses milk rather than cream means that the sweetness of its flavours is not as cloying as it might be.

1 measure/1½ tbsp Batida de Coco
1 measure/1½ tbsp crème de banane
5 measures/120ml/4fl oz full-cream (whole) milk

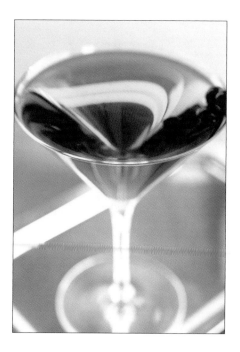

Mix the liqueurs with several ice cubes in a highball glass. Top with milk. Garnish with sliced banana and orange.

Pick-Me-Up

This is but one of the many recipes for pick-me-ups. As with all of them, it is intended to be drunk PDQ or, as Harry Craddock – Cocktail King of London's Savoy Hotel in the 1920s – used to put it, "while it's laughing at you".

1 measure/1½ tbsp dry vermouth
1 measure/1½ tbsp cherry brandy
2 dashes gin

Add the ingredients to a tumbler packed with cracked ice. Stir once, then drink.

Wally

This drink can be prepared with any apple spirit: calvados, applejack or English cider brandy. I have no idea who the gentleman was after whom it is named.

1 measure/1½ tbsp calvados
1 measure/1½ tbsp peach brandy
1 measure/1½ tbsp lime juice

Shake all the ingredients well with ice, and strain into a cocktail glass. Garnish with a thin slice of peach and a slice of lime on a cocktail stick.

Angel Face

To be dedicated to the one you love, perhaps, although after a couple of these, almost anyone will start to look good. It's another all-alcohol mix, and a pretty dry and bracing one at that, although the liqueur contributes a touch of almondy sweetness to the finish.

1 measure/1½ tbsp gin
1 measure/1½ tbsp apricot brandy
1 measure/1½ tbsp calvados

Shake all the ingredients well with ice, and strain into a cocktail glass. Garnish with a half-slice of lemon.

Tropical Cocktail

Not, as you might expect, a rum cocktail, this was the 1920s idea of tropical. In other words, it has a hint of chocolate in it. Use the brown version of crème de cacao for a less sweet result, but the attractively pale colour of the original will obviously be lost.

1 measure/1½ tbsp dry vermouth
1 measure/1½ tbsp maraschino
1 measure/1½ tbsp white crème de cacao
dash Angostura bitters
dash orange bitters (or curaçao)

Shake all the ingredients well with plenty of ice, and strain into a wine glass. Garnish with a slice of orange and a cherry.

Pink Almond

The colour of this isn't actually pink, more a sort of off-puce, but the flavour is indubitably of almond, so at least half the name is right.

1 measure/1½ tbsp Scotch
½ measure/2 tsp crème de noyau
½ measure/2 tsp kirsch
½ measure/2 tsp lemon juice
½ measure/2 tsp orgeat syrup

Shake all the ingredients well with ice, and strain into a wine goblet. Garnish with a twist of lemon and two or three slivers of flaked almond.

Green Caribbean

One of the 1980s creations that accompanied the launch of the delectable Japanese melon liqueur Midori, the name of which simply means "green". It's a supremely refreshing long drink with an appreciable kick.

Titanic

A modern recipe that should, not surprisingly, be served on a great heap of ice.

1½ measures/6 tsp vodka
1½ measures/6 tsp Mandarine Napoléon
3 measures/4½ tbsp soda water

Mix the vodka and Mandarine Napoléon with ice in a wide tumbler, and top up with soda water. Garnish with a twist of mandarin or tangerine rind.

1½ measures/6 tsp white rum
1½ measures/6 tsp Midori
4 measures/6 tbsp soda water

Shake the first two ingredients with ice, and strain into a highball glass. Add the soda and a slice of lemon.

Mad Monk

This is a cocktail I invented myself on first tasting the excellent hazelnut and herb liqueur, Frangelico, in its monk-shaped bottle.

1 measure/1½ tbsp gin
1 measure/1½ tbsp Frangelico
juice of half a lemon

Shake all the ingredients well with ice, and strain into a wine glass. You could garnish with a half-slice of lemon.

Bartending know-how
Yellow Chartreuse, formulated in 1840, is a more recent product than its green sibling. The colour of both is achieved by the natural colouring of their ingredients.

Walnut Whirl

This one sounds and, for that matter, tastes as though it ought to be lurking somewhere in the bottom layer of a box of fine chocolates.

1 measure/1½ tbsp cognac
1 measure/1½ tbsp crème de noix (walnut liqueur)
1 measure/1½ tbsp double (heavy) cream

Shake all the ingredients well with ice, and strain into a cocktail glass. Garnish with a sprinkling of grated dark chocolate and a walnut half.

Yellow Parrot

This is a powerful 1920s cocktail. It is essential to serve it over crushed ice, to mitigate a little of its firepower.

1 measure/1½ tbsp absinthe
1 measure/1½ tbsp yellow Chartreuse
1 measure/1½ tbsp apricot brandy

Shake all the ingredients well with ice, and strain into a cocktail glass filled almost to the brim with crushed ice. Do not garnish.

Eagle's Dream

The vanilla tones in purple Parfait Amour come through admirably in this foamy, gently flavoured 1920s cocktail. It should be served to your loved one on Valentine's Day, naturally.

1½ measures/6 tsp gin
1 measure/1½ tbsp Parfait Amour
juice of half a lemon
2.5ml/½ tsp caster (superfine) sugar
1 egg white

Whizz up all the ingredients with plenty of crushed ice in a blender, and strain into a large wine goblet. Garnish with a slice of lemon, or dangle a spiral twist of lemon or lime off the side of the glass, just to show you care.

Red Witch

In northern Europe and the United States, pastis is more often mixed with fruit juices than with water. Its colourlessness makes it a useful base; sharper flavours such as grapefruit are the most successful. A fashion for drinking it with blackcurrant cordial was quite the thing in Britain in the 1970s. It perhaps reminded the drinker of a certain type of childhood boiled sweet with a chewy centre that combined the flavours of liquorice and blackcurrant. Pernod and black in a tall glass topped up with sweet cider, known in the bars of the north of England as Red Witch, was a popular way of achieving oblivion in my own happily misspent youth.

Grand Slam

This is another recipe using punsch, which mixes very suavely with both shades of vermouth. Here is an aperitif cocktail, if ever there was one.

2 measures/3 tbsp punsch
1 measure/1½ tbsp dry vermouth
1 measure/1½ tbsp sweet red vermouth

Stir all the ingredients well with ice in a pitcher, and then strain over crushed ice in a wine glass. You could garnish the drink with a half-slice of orange.

Diki-Diki

I have no idea what the name of this cocktail refers to, but it was a very popular one in the Savoy American Bar in the 1920s. It is one of many from the period to use Swedish punsch.

2 measures/3 tbsp calvados
½ measure/2 tsp punsch
½ measure/2 tsp grapefruit juice

Shake all the ingredients well with ice, and strain into a cocktail glass. Add a small piece of pink grapefruit rind to the drink.

Rite of Spring

Green cocktails that don't somehow taste of mint are pretty few and far between. The relatively rare green version of curaçao is worth buying if you come across it, and here is a recipe of my own, tailor-made for it, if I say so myself.

2 measures/3 tbsp vodka
1 measure/1½ tbsp green curaçao
4 measures/6 tbsp sparkling lemonade

Mix the vodka and curaçao with ice in a pitcher until well-chilled. Pour without straining into a highball glass, and top up with the lemonade. Dangle a long twist of lemon rind in the drink.

Ojen Cocktail

This recipe was created specifically for the Spanish version of pastis, ojen. For that authentic touch, the twist should really be of the bitter Seville orange variety.

2 measures/3 tbsp dry ojen
5ml/1 tsp caster (superfine) sugar
½ measure/2 tsp still mineral water
dash orange bitters (or curaçao)

Shake all the ingredients well with ice, and strain into a small tumbler. Garnish with a twist of orange rind.

Absinthe Cocktail

This original 19th-century recipe could just be the most perfect cocktail in the world, for its simplicity and unforgettable power. Now that absinthe is widely commercially available again, it cries out to be tried. As a wise man once said, "Absinthe makes the heart grow fonder."

2 measures/3 tbsp absinthe
2 measures/3 tbsp still mineral water
dash sugar syrup
dash Angostura bitters

Shake all the ingredients well with ice, and strain into a cocktail glass. No garnish is needed. Sip slowly.

Matinée

In this nourishing, creamy, eggy mixture, the relatively small amount of Sambuca shines forth. Whip up the egg white a little before adding it to the shaker.

1 measure/1½ tbsp gin
½ measure/2 tsp Sambuca
½ measure/2 tsp double (heavy) cream
½ egg white
dash lime juice

Block and Fall

Cocktails that include pastis tend to be the most dramatic in the repertoire. Many of these contain no non-alcoholic ingredients. That is because a relatively small amount of pastis will have plenty to say for itself in even the most ferocious of mixes, concoctions that would drown the presence of many of the more delicate liqueurs.

Shake all the ingredients well with plenty of ice, and strain into a chilled cocktail glass. Sprinkle with finely grated nutmeg.

Bartending know-how
When three coffee beans are taken in a flaming Sambuca, they represent health, wealth and happiness.

1 measure/1½ tbsp cognac
1 measure/1½ tbsp Cointreau
½ measure/2 tsp Pernod
½ measure/2 tsp calvados

Stir all the ingredients together with ice in a pitcher, and then strain into a tumbler half-filled with cracked ice. Add a twist of lemon.

Drought

If you should bring back a bottle of delightful Suze from a trip to France, here is a good alternative to serving it neat. This is an unimaginably dry mixture, and a particular energizer to the appetite. It makes a fabulous lunchtime aperitif – or evening one, for that matter.

1 measure/1½ tbsp gin
1 measure/1½ tbsp Suze
dash orange juice

Shake all the ingredients well with ice, and strain into a small wine glass containing a single cube of ice. Add a little piece of orange rind.

Sundowner

This recipe uses the bitter, orange-flavoured South African liqueur, Van der Hum, in a variation on the formula for Sunburn (see below). Instead of using cognac, though, you could substitute a good South African brandy if you come across it. Many of them are surprisingly fine in quality.

1½ measures/6 tsp cognac
1 measure/1½ tbsp Van der Hum
½ measure/2 tsp orange juice
½ measure/2 tsp lemon juice

Shake all the ingredients well with ice, and strain into a cocktail glass. Garnish with a physalis fruit.

Southern Peach

The peach notes in America's classic whiskey liqueur are accentuated by its being mixed with peach brandy in this cream cocktail.

1 measure/1½ tbsp Southern Comfort
1 measure/1½ tbsp peach brandy
1 measure/1½ tbsp double (heavy) cream
dash Angostura bitters

Shake all the ingredients well with plenty of ice, and strain into a tumbler. Garnish with a wedge of ripe peach.

Sunburn

A dark and brooding combination of brandy and coffee liqueur is brightened up with fresh citrus juices. The effect is an unusual one, but you will find that you have grown to love it by the time you finish the drink.

1 measure/1½ tbsp cognac
1 measure/1½ tbsp Tia Maria
½ measure/2 tsp orange juice
½ measure/2 tsp lemon juice

Shake all the ingredients well with ice, and strain into a cocktail glass. Garnish with half-slices of orange and lemon.

Amsterdammer

Here is one of those bet-you-can't-drink-more-than-one-of-these recipes. I have never seen this on any cocktail list in Amsterdam. It seems more likely to be an American recipe.

1½ measures/6 tsp advocaat
1½ measures/6 tsp cherry brandy

Shake the ingredients very thoroughly with ice, and strain into a champagne saucer. Garnish with a cocktail cherry.

Milano

The assertive flavour of Galliano comes through strongly in this short, sour cocktail, which has a long aftertaste.

1 measure/1½ tbsp gin
1 measure/1½ tbsp Galliano

Duchess

This is a 1920s recipe in which the pungency of absinthe is tamed – if that's the right word – by a mixture of red and white vermouths.

1 measure/1½ tbsp absinthe
1 measure/1½ tbsp dry vermouth
1 measure/1½ tbsp sweet red vermouth

Shake all the ingredients well with ice, and strain into a cocktail glass. Add a small piece of lemon rind.

juice of half a lemon

Shake all the ingredients well with ice, and strain into a cocktail glass. Garnish with a cherry and slices of lemon and lime on a cocktail stick.

Saracen

This impeccably Scottish cocktail recalls the story of the Saracen's head, with which Glayva is associated. Good malt whisky is often matured in old sherry casks, so there is a Highland connection even in the use of dry sherry in the recipe.

1 measure/1½ tbsp Scotch
½ measure/2 tsp Glayva
½ measure/2 tsp pale dry (fino) sherry
dash orange bitters (or curaçao)
1 measure/1½ tbsp soda water

Shake all but the last ingredient well with ice, and pour without straining into a tumbler. Add the soda, and garnish with a piece of orange rind.

Bartending know-how
The tall fluted bottle in which Galliano is packaged is based on the classical design of Roman columns.

Strega Daiquiri

This is more or less a standard Daiquiri, in which the liqueur forms an additional element, rather than replacing the rum.

1 measure/1½ tbsp Strega
1 measure/1½ tbsp white rum
½ measure/2 tsp lemon juice
½ measure/2 tsp orange juice
2.5ml/½ tsp orgeat syrup (or sugar syrup)

Shake all the ingredients well with ice, and strain into a chilled cocktail glass. Garnish with a slice of lemon and a maraschino cherry.

Tuaca Cocktail

The combined flavours of vanilla, orange and lime in this heavenly mixture will test your moderate-drinking resolution to its limit. Once breached, you can then go on to enjoy another couple with a clear conscience.

1 measure/1½ tbsp vodka
1 measure/1½ tbsp Tuaca
½ measure/2 tsp lime juice

Shake well with ice, and strain into a cocktail glass. Garnish with orange rind.

Midori Sour

The standard Sour treatment works quite well with Midori, and certainly makes for a more exotic alternative to yet another Whisky Sour, but it's better shaken than stirred. You may well find it doesn't really need the sugar syrup.

2 measures/3 tbsp Midori
1 measure/1½ tbsp lemon juice
¼ measure/1 tsp sugar syrup

Shake well with ice, and strain into a tumbler. Garnish with a melon ball.

Café Kahlúa

This long, strong, creamy cocktail is pure self-indulgence. The addition of an optional cinnamon stick makes an imaginative alternative decoration to a plastic stirrer, and has the extra benefit of flavouring the drink as you swizzle it.

3 measures/4½ tbsp Kahlúa
1½ measures/6 tsp light rum
2 measures/3 tbsp whipping cream

Shake thoroughly with ice to incorporate the cream, and strain into a chilled tumbler. Add a stick of cinnamon.

Grand Hotel

This is a charming 1920s cocktail, the name of which may well refer to London's Savoy, one of the grandest of them all.

1½ measures/6 tsp Grand Marnier
1½ measures/6 tsp gin
½ measure/2 tsp dry vermouth
dash lemon juice

Shake all the ingredients well with ice, and strain into a large cocktail glass. Squeeze a twist of lemon over the surface and drop it into the glass.

Blue Lady

We have a Lemon Lady, a Scarlet Lady, a Pink Lady and a White Lady elsewhere, and here is their Blue sister. It's a sweet, creamy one that combines the flavours of orange and chocolate, but in a most peculiar hue.

1½ measures/6 tsp blue curaçao
½ measure/2 tsp white crème de cacao
½ measure/2 tsp double (heavy) cream

Shake thoroughly with ice, and strain into a cocktail glass. Do not garnish.

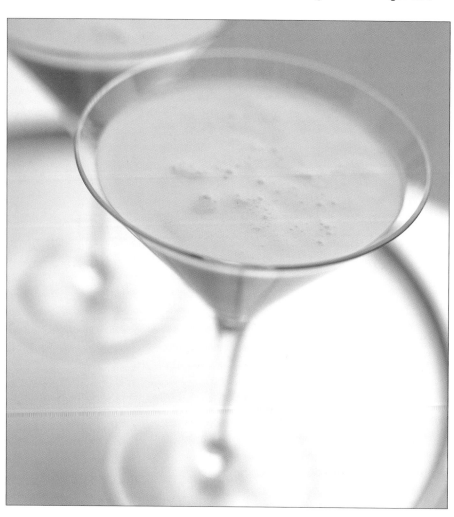

Love

This sweet old 1920s cocktail is obviously made for sharing, so the recipe below serves two.

4 measures/6 tbsp sloe gin
1 measure/1½ tbsp lemon juice
1 egg white
¼ measure/1 tsp grenadine

Shake all the ingredients well with ice and then strain into two cocktail glasses. Garnish each with a pair of cherries joined at the stalk.

Il Paradiso

Not to be confused with Paradise, this is a creamy, sumptuous, chocolate-orangey cocktail with a nice balance of sweet and bitter flavours.

1 measure/1½ tbsp Tuaca
1 measure/1½ tbsp orange curaçao
1 measure/1½ tbsp double (heavy) cream

Shake all the ingredients thoroughly with ice, and strain into a cocktail glass. Alternatively, whizz it up in the blender for an extra-frothy texture. Garnish with grated orange rind.

Bartending know-how
The credit for the formulation of the recipe on which the orangey Italian liqueur Tuaca is based is said to go to the Florentine politican Lorenzo de Medici in the 16th century – along with his many other achievements.

After-Dinner Coffee

This makes a superb Mexican-style way to end a meal. Kahlúa, the coffee liqueur used in this drink, is also delicious served in a liqueur glass topped with a thin layer of cream. This recipe serves four.

50g/2oz dark-roast ground coffee
475ml/16fl oz boiling water
120ml/4fl oz tequila
120ml/4fl oz Kahlúa
5ml/1 tsp natural vanilla essence (extract)
30ml/2 tbsp soft dark brown sugar
150ml/¼ pint double (heavy) cream

Put the ground coffee in a heatproof pitcher or cafetière, pour on the boiling water and leave until the coffee grounds settle at the bottom. Strain the coffee into a clean heatproof pitcher. Add the tequila, Kahlúa and vanilla essence to the coffee, and stir well to mix. Add the sugar and continue to stir until it has dissolved completely. Pour the mixture into small coffee cups or tall heat-resistant glasses. Hold a spoon just above the surface of each coffee. Pour the cream very slowly down the back of the spoon so that it forms a pool on top. Serve at once.

Highland Milk Punch

This is just the sort of thing to keep the cold at bay on cold nights in the frozen north, or anywhere else for that matter.

2 measures/3 tbsp Scotch
1 measure/1½ tbsp Drambuie
1 egg, beaten
250ml/8fl oz full-cream (whole) milk

Ski Lift

Here's another comforting hot drink for a rainy day. This gives ordinary drinking chocolate a real lift, and may well provide some compensation if the snow isn't good enough for skiing on.

1 measure/1½ tbsp peach schnapps
½ measure/2 tsp Malibu
hot chocolate

Make a pan of hot chocolate or cocoa in the normal way, but add the liqueurs to your mug before pouring it. Stir briskly, and top with a blob of whipped cream dusted with ground cinnamon.

Put all the ingredients into a small pan and heat gently, stirring all the time to incorporate the egg and prevent the milk from burning on the bottom of the pan. Just before the mixture boils, pour it into a mug and sprinkle the surface of the drink with powdered cinnamon.

Coffee Orloff

A John J. Poister recipe from the *New American Bartender's Guide*, this would make a very sexy after-dinner drink with a good, strong kick. Be sure to use the cream version of Grand Marnier.

¾ measure/3 tsp vodka
¾ measure/3 tsp Tia Maria
hot black coffee
¾ measure/3 tsp Crème de Grand Marnier

Add the vodka and Tia Maria to a large cup, and then top up with coffee. Pour the Crème de Grand Marnier over the back of a spoon so that it floats on top.

Café à l'Orange

This is one of numerous drink possibilities in which the flavours of orange and coffee are combined. The recipe serves four.

120ml/4fl oz whipping cream
30ml/2 tbsp icing (confectioners') sugar
5ml/1 tsp grated orange rind
600ml/1 pint hot black coffee
150ml/¼ pint any orange-flavoured liqueur, such as Grand Marnier, Cointreau, triple sec, etc
4 orange wedges, to garnish

In a clean bowl, whip the cream until stiff. Fold in the icing sugar and zest. Chill for 30 minutes, or until the cream mixture is firm enough to hold a wedge of orange on top. Divide the black coffee equally among tall glass mugs and stir about 30ml/2 tbsp liqueur into each. Top with chilled whipped cream and balance an orange wedge on top. Serve immediately.

Lisbon Flip Coffee

Here the coffee is not so much a main ingredient. It provides instead a subtle undertone to an interesting and profoundly satisfying cocktail. The recipe serves two.

4 measures/6 tbsp red port
2 measures/3 tbsp orange curaçao
1 measure/1½ tbsp very strong coffee
10ml/2 tsp icing (confectioners') sugar
2 eggs
20ml/4 tsp condensed milk
60ml/4 tbsp crushed ice
grated chocolate and orange rind shavings, to garnish

Place all the ingredients in a cocktail shaker, including the crushed ice. Shake vigorously and serve immediately in cocktail glasses. Top with the finely grated chocolate and orange rind.

African Coffee

In parts of Africa, coffee is often drunk with condensed milk. This recipe is an adaptation of an African brew with a luxurious liqueur finish.

250ml/8fl oz cold strong coffee (four generous espressos or cafetière coffee brewed using 70g/12 tbsp coffee per 1 litre/1¾ pints water)
40ml/8 tsp condensed milk
20ml/4 tsp brown crème de cacao

Shake well with ice, and strain into a tall glass half-filled with cracked ice.

Grasshopper Coffee

The name of this drink recalls the creamy crème de menthe cocktail we came across earlier, and the coffee will need to be good and strong to stand up to the flavours of the liqueurs. This recipe makes two servings.

dark and white chocolate mints
2 measures/3 tbsp green crème de menthe
2 measures/3 tbsp coffee liqueur, such as Tia Maria or Kahlúa
350ml/12fl oz hot strong black coffee
50ml/2fl oz whipping cream

Cut the dark and white chocolate mints diagonally in half. Divide the two liqueurs equally into two tall, strong latte glasses. Combine well. Fill each glass with the hot coffee and top them with whipped cream. Decorate with the chocolate mint triangles, dividing the white and dark chocolate evenly.

Easy Café Brûlot

This is a traditional coffee drink from New Orleans, where all the ingredients except the coffee are "flamed" in a bowl at the table. The flame is extinguished by pouring the coffee into the bowl. Except for the dramatic visual effects, this recipe achieves the same flavour with less fuss. It serves three to four.

3 measures/4½ tbsp brandy or rum
2 measures/3 tbsp Cointreau or other orange-flavoured liqueur
30ml/2 tbsp caster (superfine) sugar
6–8 cloves
2 sticks cinnamon
a strip of lemon and/or orange rind
700ml/24fl oz strong hot dark-roast coffee

Heat the brandy or rum, Cointreau, sugar, cloves, cinnamon sticks and lemon or orange rind in a large pan. Stir to dissolve the sugar. Pour the black coffee, brewed at about 65g/2½oz per 1 litre/1¾ pints water by the cafetière method, into the mixture. Stir and serve in coffee cups. Garnish with a cinnamon stick and orange rind.

Coffee Colada

This coffee cocktail is a riot of bold Caribbean flavours. A pitcher can be made up a couple of hours in advance, then allowed to freeze partially, before topping with plenty of whipped cream. This recipe serves four.

450ml/¾ pint cold, very strong coffee (filter/cafetière brewed using 80g/14 tbsp coffee per 1 litre/1¾ pints water)
2 measures/3 tbsp tequila (or white rum)
2 measures/3 tbsp Malibu
4 measures/6 tbsp coconut cream
2.5ml/½ tsp vanilla essence (extract)
350ml/12fl oz crushed ice
60ml/4 tbsp whipped cream and toasted coconut shavings, to garnish

Combine all the ingredients in a blender and process on a high speed. Serve in tall wine glasses. Garnish with whipped cream, topped with toasted coconut shavings.

White Hot Chocolate

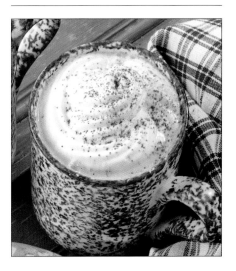

This new spin on hot chocolate matches white chocolate with orange liqueur. The recipe serves four.

1.75 litres/3 pints milk
175g/6oz white chocolate, broken into small pieces
½ measure/2 tsp coffee powder
4 measures/6 tbsp Cointreau or other orange-flavoured liqueur
whipped cream and ground cinnamon, to serve

Heat the milk in a large heavy pan until almost boiling. Remove from the heat. Add the white chocolate, coffee powder and liqueur. Stir until all the chocolate has melted. Pour into four mugs. Top each with a spoonful of whipped cream and a sprinkling of ground cinnamon. Serve immediately.

Peanut Coffee

Fans of peanut butter will love this iced drink with a coffee flavour. It's rich and filling, like a sumptuous dessert.

1½ measures/6 tsp Kahlúa
3 measures/4½ tbsp full-cream (whole) milk
30ml/2 tbsp vanilla ice cream
10ml/2 tsp smooth peanut butter
3 measures/4½ tbsp 7-Up

Put all but the last ingredient into the blender with crushed ice, and combine. Pour into a cocktail glass, and add the 7-Up. Stir once more.

Wine and champagne

Table wines are used surprisingly seldom in cocktails. That may at first seem odd, but the reason is that their flavours are so hugely various that it is difficult to give recipes that are guaranteed to come out tasting the same each time. For the following recipes, where a dry white wine is specified, go for something like a light, unoaked Chardonnay from Chile, South Africa or the south of France, and where red is used, choose something like a Côtes du Rhône or other southern French blend. When it comes to sparkling wine recipes, it isn't really worth using champagne where lots of other flavours are involved. A less expensive sparkler from another region (Australia, New Zealand, South Africa or Spain) will do quite as well.

Spritzer

The most famous white wine cocktail is this simple fizzy creation. Everyone who drinks spritzers seems to have his or her own preferred proportions, but this recipe should be reliable. The point is that the drink is lower in alcohol than a standard glass of wine.

3 measures/4½ tbsp dry white wine
4 measures/6 tbsp soda water

Half-fill a highball glass with cracked ice, and add the wine and soda. Garnish with mixed berries if you like, but the drink doesn't really need them.

Operator

Another low-alcohol preparation, Operator is to my mind a rather more satisfying drink than basic Spritzer, although along the same lines. At least it tastes of something.

2 measures/3 tbsp dry white wine
2 measures/3 tbsp sparkling ginger ale
¼ measure/1 tsp lime juice

Half-fill a rocks glass with cracked ice, and then add all the ingredients. Stir, and garnish with a slice of lime.

Crimean

You might think this would have vodka in it with a name like that, but it's actually quite innocent of the stuff. It needs straining through something like a tea-strainer in order to remove the lemon rind as well as the used ice.

2 measures/3 tbsp dry white wine
⅔ measure/1 tbsp Cointreau
grated rind of one lemon
1 measure/1½ tbsp soda water

Stir the first three ingredients well with ice in a pitcher, and strain into a rocks glass. Add the soda and garnish with a half-slice of lemon.

Fantaisie

This appealing cocktail is best made with an off-dry or medium-dry white wine, rather than the very driest. An aromatic, floral-scented Gewurztraminer from Alsace would suit the recipe down to the ground.

4 measures/6 tbsp off-dry white wine
¾ measure/3 tsp apricot brandy

Pour the wine into a well-chilled goblet. Add the liqueur and stir well. No garnish is necessary.

Sonoma Cup

The Sonoma Valley in California produces some of the world's very best Chardonnays. However, a simpler white wine will do just as well.

3 measures/4½ tbsp dry white wine
½ measure/2 tsp Cointreau

3 measures/4½ tbsp orange juice
4 measures/6 tbsp soda water

Shake all but the last ingredient well with ice, and strain into a highball glass. Add the soda, stir gently and garnish with a half-slice of orange.

Waltzing Matilda

A longer, stronger drink than most white wine cocktails, the name of this cocktail suggests that an Australian Chardonnay would be the best wine to use. If so, go for an unoaked one, as anything else will probably be too overwhelming for the mixture. Even the simplest wines should have a ripe, buttery flavour.

4 measures/6 tbsp dry white wine
1 measure/1½ tbsp gin
1½ measures/6 tsp passion fruit juice
¼ measure/1 tsp orange curaçao
3 measures/4½ tbsp sparkling ginger ale

Shake all but the last ingredient well with ice, and strain into a highball glass. Add the ginger ale and a lemon slice.

Sangria

Testament to the Spanish influence on Mexican cooking, this popular thirst-quencher is traditionally served in large pitchers, with ice and citrus fruit slices floating on top. This recipe serves six.

750ml/1¼ pints red wine
juice of 2 limes
4 measures/6 tbsp orange juice
4 measures/6 tbsp brandy
50g/2oz caster (superfine) sugar
1 lime, sliced, to garnish

Combine the wine, lime juice, orange juice and brandy in a large glass pitcher. Stir in the sugar until it has dissolved completely. Serve in tall glasses with ice. Garnish each glass with a slice of lime.

English Christmas Punch

This old Victorian recipe for a red wine punch uses tea. It may not taste like any punch you've previously been used to, but it makes a properly festive tipple. It would once have contained about twice this quantity of sugar, so add more if you think the resulting mixture isn't sweet enough. The recipe makes about 24 servings.

2 bottles red wine
3 teacups strong tea
juice of an orange
juice of a lemon
225g/8 oz caster (superfine) sugar
a 700ml/1 pint bottle dark rum
orange and lemon slices, to garnish

Heat the wine, tea and fruit juices in a pan, without allowing them to boil. Simmer for about 5 minutes, and then add the sugar, stirring until it has all dissolved. Transfer to a punchbowl. Using the same pan, heat about a quarter of the rum until it starts seething and set it alight. Pour the flaming rum into the punchbowl, and then add the rest of the rum. Stir well, and throw in some orange and lemon slices.

Bordeaux Cocktail

A good way of disguising any harshness in a young red wine, this recipe is classically made with a young claret from Bordeaux. Wine-tasters claim to find the taste of blackcurrant in the Cabernet Sauvignon grape that most claret contains, but you can make sure of that by adding the blackcurrant liqueur, cassis.

2 measures/3 tbsp red Bordeaux
1 measure/1½ tbsp cognac
¾ measure/3 tsp crème de cassis

Stir all the ingredients well with ice in a pitcher, and strain into a large wine glass. Do not garnish.

Mulled Red Wine

This is an excellent warm drink to serve on a cold winter's evening (at Christmas, traditionally), as it will really get the party started. The word "mulled" is derived from an old English dialect word of the late 14th or early 15th century, meaning "mixed" or "muddled", which is how you may feel after over-indulging in it. Then again it might only mull you into a false sense of security. This recipe serves six.

1 bottle red wine
75g/3oz soft light brown sugar
2 cinnamon sticks
1 lemon, sliced
4 whole cloves
150ml/¼ pint brandy or port

Put all the ingredients, except the brandy or port, into a large pan. Bring the wine to the boil to dissolve the sugar. Remove immediately, cover the pan and leave it to stand for 5 minutes, allowing the flavours to infuse. Strain to remove the spices and lemon slices. Add the brandy and serve warm, with a fresh slice of lemon in each glass.

Royal Silver

A sparkling wine cocktail should always look grand, and this one benefits from the frosted red rim given to the glass.

½ measure/2 tsp Poire William
½ measure/2 tsp Cointreau
1½ measures/6 tsp pink grapefruit juice
champagne or sparkling wine

Frost the rim of a large wine goblet by dipping it into grenadine and then caster (superfine) sugar. Shake the first three ingredients well with ice, and strain into the prepared glass. Top up with champagne or sparkling wine, and garnish with a chunk of ripe pear and a half-slice of orange on a cocktail stick.

Champagne Cocktail

The original champagne cocktail is an American recipe dating from the 19th century, although nobody appears to know precisely when it was first invented. It certainly makes a change from serving champagne straight, but I would only use a relatively inexpensive, non-vintage wine. As a rule, the very best stuff should never be mixed.

1 sugar cube
2 dashes Angostura bitters
¼ measure/1 tsp cognac
champagne

Drop the sugar cube into a champagne flute, and add the Angostura, rolling the sugar lump to soak it. Pour in the brandy, and then top the glass up with freshly opened champagne.

Marilyn Monroe

The drink named in honour of one of the great screen sirens of all time should really be made not just with champagne, but with the premium brand Dom Pérignon. It is fearfully expensive, though. Moët & Chandon Brut Impérial, made by the same house, might suffice instead.

4 measures/6 tbsp well-chilled champagne
1 measure/1½ tbsp applejack or calvados
¼ measure/1 tsp grenadine

Add all the ingredients to a champagne saucer, and give the drink the gentlest of stirs. Garnish with a couple of cocktail cherries.

Night and Day

This is an elegant recipe full of complementary flavours. The mixture should not be stirred, so that the layers of different drinks come at the drinker one by one.

3 measures/4½ tbsp champagne or sparkling
    wine
¾ measure/3 tsp cognac
½ measure/2 tsp Grand Marnier
¼ measure/1 tsp Campari

Add the ingredients in this order to a large wine goblet filled with crushed ice.

Sparkling Peach Melba

This refreshing fruit fizz is an excellent choice for summer celebrations. As with most soft fruit recipes, its success depends on using the ripest, tastiest peaches and raspberries available. This recipe serves four.

3 ripe peaches
90ml/6 tbsp orange juice
75g/3oz raspberries
10ml/2 tsp icing (confectioners') sugar
about 500ml/17fl oz raspberry sorbet
about 400ml/14fl oz medium sparkling
  wine, chilled

Put the peaches in a heatproof bowl and cover with boiling water. Leave for a minute, then drain and peel off the skins. Cut the fruit in half and remove the stones. Chop the peach halves roughly, and purée them with the orange juice in a blender until smooth. Transfer to a bowl.

Put the raspberries in the blender with the icing sugar, and process until smooth. Press the raspberry purée through a sieve into a separate bowl. Chill both purées for at least an hour.

Spoon the chilled peach purée into four tall glasses. Add scoops of sorbet to fill the glasses. Spoon the raspberry purée around the sorbet. Top up each glass with sparkling wine. Garnish with mint sprigs.

Buck's Fizz

Hugely popular in the 1980s, Buck's Fizz is a simple mixture of two-thirds champagne to one-third orange juice; it is not half and half, as is often suggested. It is a 1920s recipe invented at a club called Buck's in London. Some recipes add ¼ measure/1 tsp grenadine to it, to deepen the colour, but it isn't necessary. It is best served in flute glasses, but you can use a large wine goblet instead if you want to appear more generous.

Mustique

This rum drink was invented on the Caribbean island of Mustique.

1 measure/1½ tbsp light rum
1 measure/1½ tbsp orange juice
½ measure/2 tsp lemon juice
¼ measure/1 tsp grenadine
champagne or sparkling wine

Shake all but the last ingredient with ice, and strain into a large wine glass. Top with fizz, and garnish with a half-slice of lemon.

Blackberry and Champagne Crush

This sparkling blend makes a good brunch alternative to Buck's Fizz. For a party, divide the blackberry purée among six glasses and top up with champagne. This recipe, though, is just for two.

175g/6oz blackberries
15ml/1 tbsp icing (confectioners') sugar
30ml/2 tbsp cognac
250ml/8fl oz champagne or sparkling wine,
  chilled

Purée the blackberries in a food processor. Push the purée through a sieve, and then add the sugar. Pour the brandy into two glasses. Return the blackberry purée to the food processor, add the sparkling wine and blend for no more than two or three seconds. Pour into the glasses and serve immediately.

Bocuse Special

This recipe was created by the French master-chef Paul Bocuse at his restaurant in the south of France.

½ measure/2 tsp crème de cassis
½ measure/2 tsp crème de framboise
champagne

Mix the liqueurs together with ice in a small pitcher until well-chilled. Strain into a flute glass, and top up with champagne. Drop a raspberry into the glass if you have one to hand.

Southern Champagne

This is how they like a champagne cocktail in the southern states of America.

1 measure/1½ tbsp Southern Comfort
dash Angostura bitters
ice-cold champagne or sparkling wine

Add the liqueur and bitters to a champagne flute. Mix briefly and top up with champagne or sparkling wine. Squeeze a small twist of orange rind over the drink, and then drop it into the glass.

B2 C2

The story goes that American troops advancing through Germany in 1945 stumbled on a wine merchant's premises, and cobbled together their own cocktail from whatever came to hand. The name refers of course to the initials of the four ingredients.

1 measure/1½ tbsp brandy (cognac)
1 measure/1½ tbsp Bénédictine
1 measure/1½ tbsp Cointreau
4 measures/6 tbsp well-chilled champagne

Add the ingredients in this order to a large wine goblet. No garnish is necessary.

Pizzetti

This charming cocktail was created at a hotel in the Cortina region of Italy, and its name literally means "little pizzas". You work it out.

1 measure/1½ tbsp cognac
2 measures/3 tbsp orange juice
2 measures/3 tbsp grapefruit juice
champagne or sparkling wine

Shake the first three ingredients well with ice, and strain into a chilled wine goblet. Top up with champagne or sparkling wine, and stir gently. Garnish with a cherry.

Fortified wines

The most resourceful fortified wine of all for cocktail-making is vermouth. Whether in its dry white or sweet red version, its aromatic, herbal flavours equip it handsomely for mixing with any of the spirits and a fair few of the liqueurs. We shouldn't forget the other fortified wines, though: those that haven't had herbs infused in them, but are basically ordinary table wines boosted with the addition of grape spirit. Sherry and port are used quite widely, and I have even managed to track down a couple of recipes that use madeira and Marsala.

Gin and It

The name of this drink is a shortened form of gin and Italian, so-called in the days when Italian vermouths were inaccurately thought to be always of the sweet red variety. (By the same token, gin and dry vermouth was known as Gin and French.) Proportions vary according to individual taste, and many recipes show the gin and vermouth in equal quantities. This is my preference.

2 measures/3 tbsp gin
1 measure/1½ tbsp sweet red vermouth

Add both ingredients to a rocks glass with a couple of ice cubes in it. Stir, and add a twist of lemon rind.

Bronx

An utterly satisfying mixture of gin and both vermouths, Bronx is basically a sort of gin Manhattan with a little orange juice. It is, naturally, a New York cocktail that dates back to the early years of the 20th century. Like all such mixtures, it makes a very effective aperitif.

1½ measures/6 tsp gin
¾ measure/3 tsp dry vermouth
¾ measure/3 tsp sweet red vermouth
juice of a quarter of an orange

Shake all the ingredients well with ice, and strain into a cocktail glass. Garnish with a half-slice of orange.

Bentley

Dubonnet has one of the most captivating flavours of all vermouth brands, derived in part from its long maturation in cask. Unless otherwise stated, these recipes call for the red version. Bentley is a fine aperitif mixture dating from the 1920s.

1½ measures/6 tsp calvados
1½ measures/6 tsp Dubonnet

Shake well with ice, and strain into a glass. Garnish with an orange twist.

Boston

This is another egg recipe containing a little sugar too, although the underlying mixture is quite dry.

1½ measures/6 tsp dry (sercial) madeira
1½ measures/6 tsp bourbon

Coronation

The Coronation for which this cocktail was created was that of George V in 1910. It's a strong, forthright mixture, much like King George himself.

1 measure/1½ tbsp sweet red vermouth
1 measure/1½ tbsp dry vermouth
1 measure/1½ tbsp calvados
¼ measure/1 tsp apricot brandy

Shake all the ingredients well with ice, and strain into a cocktail glass. Garnish with a half-slice of orange.

2.5ml/½ tsp caster (superfine) sugar
1 egg yolk

Shake all the ingredients with ice and strain into a small wine glass. Sprinkle with grated nutmeg.

Golf

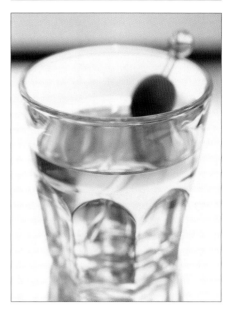

This is an old 1920s recipe for a very short drink that is a distant relation of the Martini. It was indeed originally known as the Golf Martini, but is clearly for those who like a little more vermouth with their gin.

1 measure/1½ tbsp gin
½ measure/2 tsp dry vermouth
2 dashes Angostura bitters

Stir all the ingredients well with ice in a small pitcher, and strain into a tumbler. Garnish with a green olive.

Bartending know-how
Vermouth comes in a variety of styles. The red is made with red wine; the dry white gains an amber tinge from ageing in oak casks; bianco is sweetened-up dry white; the pink version is based on rosé wine.

Lily

Lillet is an aromatized, bittersweet, French fortified wine that comes in both red and white versions. It's hard to find now. It obviously bestowed its name (more or less) on this cocktail, but if you can't find it, use ordinary dry white vermouth instead.

1 measure/1½ tbsp gin
1 measure/1½ tbsp white Lillet or dry vermouth
1 measure/1½ tbsp crème de noyau
dash lemon juice

Shake all the ingredients well with ice, and strain into a wine glass. Garnish with a half-slice of lemon.

Midsummer Night

The orangey, quinine flavour of Italian Punt e Mes goes well with gin and a modest amount of blackcurrant liqueur in this modern recipe.

1 measure/1½ tbsp gin

1 measure/1½ tbsp Punt e Mes
½ measure/2 tsp crème de cassis

Shake all the ingredients well with ice, and strain into a cocktail glass. You could garnish with a twist of lemon.

Devil's Cocktail

For some reason, this old cocktail has come to be given the Spanish name, Diablo, in modern bar books, but the mixture remains essentially the same. It was probably originally made with red port, but white produces a more harmonious result.

1½ measures/6 tsp dry vermouth
1½ measures/6 tsp white port
2 dashes lemon juice

Shake all the ingredients well with ice, and strain into a cocktail glass. Garnish with a twist of lemon.

Breakfast

Save a tiny quantity of egg white before you scramble your breakfast eggs, and this cocktail might well make a good accompaniment to them. Then again, it would make a much better nightcap.

2 measures/3 tbsp red port
1 measure/1½ tbsp brown crème de cacao
¼ measure/1 tsp light rum
½ measure/2 tsp lemon juice
5ml/1 tsp egg white

Shake all the ingredients well with ice, and strain into a wine glass. Dust the surface with ground nutmeg.

Perfect Cocktail

Another gin and vermouths recipe from the 1920s, this is a little like Bronx, but without the orange juice. Then again, substitute Pernod for the gin and you have a Duchess.

1 measure/1½ tbsp gin
1 measure/1½ tbsp dry vermouth
1 measure/1½ tbsp sweet red vermouth

Shake all the ingredients well with ice, and strain into a cocktail glass. Garnish with a twist of lemon rind.

Bartending know-how
Use an LBV port if you can, in preference to plain ruby.

Bamboo

An exceedingly dry aperitif cocktail, with a slight bittering element, this makes a change from the usual neat dry sherry. One or two recipes add sweet red vermouth to it too, but that really is missing the point. If you have it, you could use orange bitters instead of the Angostura version.

Sloppy Joe

Strong and exotic, this is an American recipe of the postwar years. Some suggest adding 2.5ml/½ tsp grenadine to the mixture, but it doesn't really make much difference.

1 measure/1½ tbsp red port
1 measure/1½ tbsp cognac
2 measures/3 tbsp pineapple juice
2 dashes Cointreau

Shake all the ingredients well with ice, and strain into a wine goblet. Garnish with a half-slice of orange.

2 measures/3 tbsp pale dry (fino) sherry
2 measures/3 tbsp dry vermouth
2 dashes Angostura bitters

Stir all the ingredients well with ice, and strain into a large, chilled cocktail glass. You could garnish the drink with a twist of lemon.

First Avenue

A fine, slightly effervescent cocktail that uses one of the sweeter styles of sherry. Use decent oloroso, though, rather than cream sherry.

1½ measures/6 tsp sweet (oloroso) sherry
½ measure/2 tsp Cointreau
¾ measure/3 tsp soda water
¼ measure/1 tsp Campari

Half-fill a rocks glass with cracked ice. Add the first two ingredients and stir well. Add the soda, and then float the Campari on top. Do not garnish.

Prairie Oyster

I'm cheating a little by including this most challenging of hangover cures here, largely because it was once common in America to substitute sweet madeira for the brandy in a Prairie Oyster. If you're a stickler for tradition, use cognac, but you might find this a touch less aggressive if you are resorting to the drink medicinally.

1 measure/1½ tbsp sweet (malmsey)
    madeira, or cognac
¼ measure/1 tsp white wine vinegar
¼ measure/1 tsp Worcestershire sauce
pinch cayenne pepper
dash Tabasco
1 egg yolk

Add the first five ingredients to a small tumbler. Mix well without ice, and then spoon the yolk very gently on top. The preparation should then be swallowed in one gulp, without breaking the yolk.

Casanova

Marsala, from the island of Sicily, comes in various styles, but everyone seems agreed that the sweet version, dolce, is the best. That's what's used in this strong cream cocktail.

1 measure/1½ tbsp bourbon
½ measure/2 tsp Marsala dolce

Downhill

The name of this drink reflects pretty much where you'll be going if you try to take more than one. It's a knee-trembling, all-alcohol cocktail for the truly intrepid.

1 measure/1½ tbsp sweet (oloroso) sherry
½ measure/2 tsp gin
½ measure/2 tsp dry vermouth
½ measure/2 tsp orange curaçao
¼ measure/1 tsp cognac

Stir the ingredients with ice in a pitcher to chill them, and strain into a rocks glass half-filled with cracked ice. Add an orange twist and a cherry.

½ measure/2 tsp Kahlúa
1 measure/1½ tbsp double (heavy) cream

Shake all the ingredients well with plenty of ice to amalgamate the cream, and strain into a cocktail glass. Sprinkle the top with ground nutmeg.

Third Rail

There isn't much call for the peppermint cordial that was once used in this American cocktail. If you can't get hold of it, use the white version of crème de menthe instead. It ups the alcohol ante of the drink, but only just.

3 measures/4½ tbsp dry vermouth
¼ measure/1 tsp orange curacao
¼ measure/1 tsp peppermint cordial

Stir all the ingredients well with ice in a pitcher, and strain into a chilled cocktail glass. Squeeze a piece of lemon rind over the drink, and then drop it into the glass.

Marsala Cocktail

This is my own preferred way of showing Marsala to its best advantage if you don't want to drink it straight. The teaspoon of spirit and dash of acidity mingle very subtly with its toffee sweetness.

2 measures/3 tbsp Marsala dolce
¼ measure/1 tsp cognac
dash lemon juice

Stir well with ice in a pitcher, and strain into a wine glass. Add a cube of ice.

Port Cocktail

Here is another very simple preparation that goes back a long way. Like the Sherry Cocktail, it uses a hint of orange.

2 measures/3 tbsp good red port (LBV)
dash cognac

Stir the ingredients well with ice in a small pitcher until quite cold, and strain into a wine glass. Squeeze a piece of orange rind over the drink so that plenty of its oil is released, but don't put it in.

Sherry Cocktail

This was very popular in the 1920s as a sophisticated aperitif, and deserves to be so now too.

2 measures/3 tbsp pale dry (fino or manzanilla) sherry
¼ measure/1 tsp dry vermouth
¼ measure/1 tsp orange bitters (or curaçao)

Stir all the ingredients with plenty of ice in a pitcher, and strain into a large wine glass. Do not garnish.

Dubonnet Cocktail

A quartet of recipes named after four of the basic fortified wine types concludes with this one using the French proprietary classic. Be sure to use the red version.

1½ measures/6 tsp gin
1½ measures/6 tsp Dubonnet

Shake both ingredients well with ice, and strain into a small wine goblet. Squeeze a twist of lemon rind over the drink and drop it in.

Adonis

If you don't care for the sweetness of sweet sherry, go for this 1920s recipe. A dry style is given the herbal sweetness of red vermouth instead.

2 measures/3 tbsp pale dry (fino) sherry
1 measure/1½ tbsp sweet red vermouth
2 dashes orange bitters (or curaçao)

Stir all the ingredients well with ice in a pitcher, and strain into a wine glass. Garnish with a twist of orange rind.

Sherry Flip

The recipe for a Flip would seem to go back to the 17th century, in that a mixture of alcohol, sugar and egg was being made then. In the pre-cocktail-shaker era, they were mixed by being repeatedly poured, or "flipped", between two glasses. A version using sweet sherry has proved the most enduringly popular of them all. The nutmeg is de rigueur.

Straight Law

This century-old recipe is as straight as they come. Both the ingredients are very dry and very strong in flavour. It's a real appetite awakener.

2 measures/3 tbsp pale dry (fino) sherry
1 measure/1½ tbsp gin

Stir both ingredients well with ice, and strain into a cocktail glass. Squeeze a piece of lemon rind over the surface and drop it into the drink.

2 measures/3 tbsp brown cream sherry
2.5ml/½ tsp caster (superfine) sugar
1 egg, beaten

Shake all the ingredients well with ice, and strain into a small wine glass. Sprinkle grated nutmeg on the surface. Alternatively, you can whizz it up in the blender if quite convenient.

Merry Widow

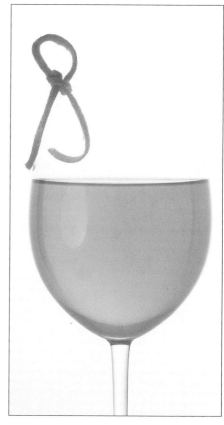

This is another 1920s recipe, this time at the bone-dry end of the spectrum, notwithstanding that splash of Bénédictine. It's a strong one too, all alcohol, which explains the merriness of the widow.

1 measure/1½ tbsp gin
1 measure/1½ tbsp dry vermouth
2 dashes absinthe
2 dashes Bénédictine
2 dashes Angostura bitters

Stir all the ingredients well with ice in a pitcher, and then strain into a large wine glass. Squeeze a twist of lemon rind over the drink, and then drop it in.

Havana Cobbler

This is an old-fashioned drink that is delightfully refreshing served in sultry, Caribbean-type weather, or in an English summer, at a push.

¼ measure/1 tsp sugar syrup
½ measure/2 tsp green ginger wine
1 measure/1½ tbsp light rum (preferably Cuban)
1 measure/1½ tbsp red port

Shake the first three ingredients well with ice, and strain into a chilled short tumbler. Tilt the glass, and slowly pour the port down the side to form a floating layer on top of the cocktail.

Bartending know-how
Stone's Special Reserve is the most gingery ginger wine of them all.

Parkeroo

This is a dry and rather startling mixture, which is worth trying at least once, just so you can say you have. I can't say it's one of my own favourites, but who's asking?

2 measures/3 tbsp pale dry (fino) sherry
1 measure/1½ tbsp tequila

Mix both ingredients in a pitcher with ice. Strain into a champagne flute filled with shaved ice, and add a twist of lemon rind.

Inigo Jones

Here is the only cocktail in this book to use rosé wine. Choose one from a southern-hemisphere country such as South Africa or Argentina. These wines tend to be much fruitier than the European ones, and you will of course have to finish the bottle straight after you've made this cocktail.

1 measure/1½ tbsp marsala dolce
1 measure/1½ tbsp dry rosé wine
1 measure/1½ tbsp cognac
dash orange juice
dash lemon juice

In a pitcher, stir together all the ingredients with plenty of ice. Strain into a tumbler half-filled with crushed ice. Garnish with a slice of orange.

Port in a Storm

I have always loved this poetically named cocktail, in which the port does indeed get buffeted by a storm of other ingredients.

2 measures/3 tbsp red wine
1½ measures/6 tsp red port
½ measure/2 tsp cognac

Stir all the ingredients with plenty of ice in a pitcher, and pour without straining into a large wine glass. You could garnish with a half-slice of orange.

Nightmare Abbey

Despite sounding like an adaptation of a Gothic novel starring Vincent Price, this mixture is perfectly sweet-natured.

1½ measures/6 tsp red Dubonnet
1 measure/1½ tbsp gin
1 measure/1½ tbsp orange juice
¾ measure/3 tsp cherry brandy

Shake all the ingredients well with ice, and strain into a bowl-shaped cocktail glass. Garnish with a twist of orange rind and a black cherry.

Soul Kiss

This fine American cocktail productively brings together three good fortified wines with orange to bind them.

1 measure/1½ tbsp red Dubonnet
1 measure/1½ tbsp sweet red vermouth
1 measure/1½ tbsp dry vermouth
1 measure/1½ tbsp orange juice

Shake all the ingredients well with ice, and strain into a large wine goblet. Garnish with a half-slice of orange.

Caffè Vermouth

Vermouth is not an obvious choice to partner coffee, but the resulting flavour is good: original and sophisticated. This recipe serves two.

4 measures/6 tbsp sweet red vermouth
60ml/4 tbsp very strong cold coffee (espresso strength or filter/cafetière brewed at 75g/3oz coffee per 1 litre/1¾ pints water)
250ml/8fl oz milk
10ml/2 tsp caster (superfine) sugar

Shake all the ingredients well with ice, and strain into cocktail glasses or tumblers. Garnish with a few roasted coffee beans.

Bartending know-how
Madeira is the hardiest of the fortified wines. An opened bottle will keep for years without declining.

Funchal Flip

This cocktail is named after Funchal, the capital of the island of Madeira, where some of the best fortified wines in the world are made.

1 measure/1½ tbsp sweet madeira
¾ measure/3 tsp cognac
½ measure/2 tsp Cointreau
¼ measure/1 tsp grenadine
1 egg yolk, beaten

Shake all the ingredients well with ice, and strain into a cocktail glass. Garnish with a half-slice of orange and a cherry.

Tinton

A traditional 1920s formula named after some long-forgotten worthy, this cocktail gives a sweet kick to apple brandy for those who find it too dry as it comes. It could be taken as an after-dinner digestif.

2 measures/3 tbsp calvados
1 measure/1½ tbsp red port

Shake both ingredients well with ice, and strain into a cocktail glass. There is no need for any garnish.

Dubonnet Fizz

This American recipe makes for a sweetly aromatic cocktail. High rollers might fill it up with champagne, but soda will do quite nicely, thank you.

4 measures/6 tbsp red Dubonnet
½ measure/2 tsp cherry brandy
2 measures/3 tbsp orange juice

Wine Collins

The wine named here is the fortified variety. Port, sweet madeira or marsala dolce can all be used as the base for this fizzy drink, but be generous.

4 measures/6 tbsp red port, malmsey
    madeira or marsala dolce
½ measure/2 tsp lime juice
sparkling lemonade

Add the first two ingredients to a highball glass half-filled with cracked ice, and stir well. Top up with lemonade, and garnish with a slice of lemon and a cherry.

1 measure/1½ tbsp lemon juice
soda water or champagne

Shake all but the last ingredient well with ice, and strain into a highball glass. Top up with soda water or champagne. You could garnish the drink with half-slices of orange and lemon.

Reform

Invented at the Reform Club at London in the 1920s, this cocktail is – as eagle-eyed drinkers will note – essentially a dry version of Adonis.

2 measures/3 tbsp pale dry (fino) sherry
1 measure/1½ tbsp dry vermouth
dash orange bitters (or curaçao)

Stir all the ingredients well with ice in a pitcher, and strain into a cocktail glass. Garnish with a cherry.

Bartending know-how
Pale dry sherry should always be treated with kid gloves. It needs drinking within a few days of the bottle being broached, and should always be served well-chilled. More than any other drink in this book, it is served in sub-standard condition in many bars and restaurants.

Beer and cider

Beer and cider are the least used of all alcoholic drinks in cocktails. They do come in handy for punches and mulled ale recipes, but as ingredients in short mixed drinks, they have only a limited number of applications. Probably the simplest beer "cocktail" of them all is shandy, which is roughly equal measures of beer and lemonade, and is always worth making for yourself, as opposed to resorting to one of the bottled proprietary brands. Good cider is one of the glories of the English brewing industry, as was once the now-forgotten perry, a refreshing sparkling drink made from pears.

Lamb's Wool

A kind of 17th-century punch, this was traditionally drunk on All Saints' Day, November 1. This recipe serves four.

1 litre/1¾ pints English bitter ale
4 baked apples
2.5ml/½ tsp ground nutmeg
2.5ml/½ tsp ground ginger
60g/2oz sugar

Heat the ale gently in a large pan without boiling it. When the apples have finished baking in the oven, peel them, remove the cores and mash the soft flesh with a potato masher. Stir the apple into the beer with the spices and sugar, and serve in warm glasses or mugs. It's a real treat that will warm you up on a dark autumn day.

Black Velvet

This simple but mightily effective drink was invented at Brooks' Club in London in 1861, following the death of Queen Victoria's husband, Prince Albert. It was considered an appropriate sign of mourning to dress the champagne up in black livery. As a popular mixture ever since, it has an appeal all its own.

Half-fill a tall, narrow beer glass with Guinness. Wait for the head to settle, and then without tilting the glass, gently top it up with good brut champagne.

Devon Gin

This is a short individual drink that will prove peculiarly potent on a cold winter's day. Tread warily.

3 measures/4½ tbsp strong sweet cider
¾ measure/3 tsp gin
¼ measure/1 tsp Cointreau

Half-fill a rocks glass with cracked ice, and add the first two ingredients, Stir gently, and then pour the Cointreau carefully on to the surface to form a float. Drink quickly.

Wassail Bowl

The wassail bowl was a wide-mouthed bowl from which hot punches were drunk. Cheer your Christmas carol-singers by offering them a bowl (or mug) each of this warming, festive drink. The recipe serves six.

2 litres/3½ pints strong bitter or brown ale
150ml/¼ pint brown cream sherry
90g/3oz caster (superfine) sugar
5ml/1 tsp ground nutmeg
5ml/1 tsp ground ginger
6 baked apples

Heat the beer, sherry, sugar and spices in a pan until gently simmering, stirring to dissolve the sugar. After about 5 minutes, decant the mixture into mugs or drinking bowls, each containing a whole mashed apple. Serve with spoons for stirring it up as it is drunk.

Cider Cup

A cup makes an excellent long and refreshing drink for an aperitif or party starter. It should be prepared shortly before serving so that the ice doesn't have time to melt. This recipe serves six.

rind of 1 lemon
slices of orange
5 measures/120ml/4fl oz pale dry (fino) sherry
3 measures/4½ tbsp cognac
3 measures/4½ tbsp white curaçao
2 measures/3 tbsp amaretto
600ml/1 pint good-quality strong dry cider

Partially fill a pitcher with cracked ice and stir in the lemon rind and the orange slices. Add the sherry, brandy, curaçao and amaretto, and stir well to mix. Pour in the cider and stir gently. Serve the cocktail in chilled tall glasses, including some of the citrus fruit in each one, and add a twist of cucumber rind.

Somerset Punch

This is a very appealing cider punch for serving at a garden party. The recipe makes around 14–16 servings.

1 litre/1¾ pints strong dry cider
150ml/¼ pint dry white wine
2 measures/3 tbsp cider brandy
150ml/¼ pint orange juice
2 measures/3 tbsp lemon juice
150ml/¼ pint pressed apple juice (not from concentrate)
300ml/½ pint sparkling ginger ale

Mix all the ingredients with ice in a punchbowl, and decant into wine glasses for serving. Garnish with thin slices of unpeeled apple.

Bartending know-how
The best ciders are those that come in a bottle with a champagne-style cork. They may be cloudy, but the quality is incomparable.

Non-alcoholic drinks

Not every cocktail session has to involve intoxication. There will be times, such as when dealing with a party of drivers, or in the course of a detox diet, or even in the middle of a raging hot day, when an alcoholic drink is not what's wanted. The non-alcoholic section of many cocktail books often has an air of "These are the also-rans" about it. That is not so here. There are enough recipes in the following pages to keep even the most determined mixologist going for a fair old time and, even more than their alcohol-based cousins, these drinks can be freely adapted as you see fit. Let your imagination off the leash.

Horse's Fall

This is a long drink to serve on a summer's day. The addition of strongly flavoured tea is a matter of taste.

1 lemon
dash Angostura bitters
2 measures/3 tbsp raspberry, Orange Pekoe
  or Assam tea, chilled (optional)
1 measure/1½ tbsp unsweetened apple juice
5 measures/120ml/4fl oz dry ginger ale or
  lemonade

Cut the rind from the lemon in one continuous strip and use it to line and decorate a long cocktail glass. Chill the glass until needed. Add a dash of Angostura to the bottom of the glass. Measure the tea, if using, into the cocktail shaker and add the apple juice. Shake for about 20 seconds. Strain into the prepared chilled glass. Finish with ginger ale or lemonade straight from the refrigerator, to taste.

Sunburst

Bursting with freshness and vitamins, this drink is a good early morning pick-me-up. This recipe makes two.

1 green apple, cored and chopped
3 carrots, peeled and chopped
1 mango, peeled and pitted
7 measures/150ml/¼ pint orange juice, chilled
6 strawberries, hulled

Place the apple, carrots and mango in a blender or food processor and process to a pulp. Add the orange juice and strawberries and process again. Strain well through a sieve, pressing out all the juice with the back of a wooden spoon. Discard any pulp left in the sieve. Pour into tumblers filled with ice cubes and serve immediately, garnished with a slice of orange on the side of the glass.

Virgin Prairie Oyster

This superior pick-me-up is a variation on the Bloody Mary. The tomato base can be drunk without the raw egg yolk if it does not appeal to you. Use only fresh free-range eggs.

175ml/6fl oz tomato juice
½ measure/2 tsp Worcestershire sauce
¼–½ measure/1–2 tsp balsamic vinegar
1 egg yolk
cayenne pepper, to taste

Measure the tomato juice into a large bar glass and stir over plenty of ice until well chilled. Strain into a tall tumbler half-filled with ice cubes. Add the Worcestershire sauce and balsamic vinegar to taste and mix with a swizzle-stick. Float the egg yolk on top and lightly dust with cayenne pepper.

Scarlet Lady

On the first sip, with its fruity and fresh tones, this drink could fool a fair few into thinking it was an alcoholic wine-based cocktail.

125g/4oz cubed melon, preferably Galia or Canteloupe
5 small red seedless grapes
3 measures/4½ tbsp unsweetened red grape juice

Fruit and Ginger Ale

This is an old English mulled drink, served chilled over ice. Of course it can be made with ready-squeezed apple and orange juices, but roasting the fruit with cloves gives a much better flavour. This recipe makes four to six servings.

1 cooking apple
1 orange, scrubbed
1 lemon, scrubbed
20 whole cloves
7.5cm/3in piece fresh ginger, peeled
30g/1oz light brown sugar
375ml/13fl oz bitter lemon

Put the melon and grapes in a blender and process until they form a smooth purée. Add the red grape juice and continue to process for another minute. Strain the juice into a bar glass of ice and stir until chilled. Pour into a chilled cocktail glass. Dip some red, seedless grapes in the lightly beaten white of an egg, and then into 15ml/1 tbsp sugar. Thread on to a cocktail stick to garnish.

Preheat the oven to 200°C/400°F/Gas 6. Score the apple around the middle and stud the orange and lemon with the cloves. Bake the fruits in the oven for about 25 minutes, until soft and completely cooked through. Quarter the orange and lemon, and mash the apple, discarding the peel and the core.

Finely grate the ginger. Place the fruit and ginger in a bowl with the light brown sugar. Add 300ml/½ pint boiling water. Using a spoon, squeeze the fruit to release more flavour. Cover and let sit for an hour until cool. Strain into a pitcher of cracked ice and use a spoon to press out all the juices from the fruit. Add the bitter lemon. Garnish with orange wedges and whole cloves.

Volunteer

This drink is ideal for a lazy summer afternoon. It's also a fine cocktail to serve the designated driver at a party. It was devised and drunk during a very rough Channel crossing in an undersized boat, a tribute to human resourcefulness!

2 measures/3 tbsp lime cordial
2–3 dashes Angostura bitters
7 measures/150ml/¼ pint chilled tonic water
decorative ice cubes, to serve

Pour the lime cordial into the bottom of the glass, and shake in the Angostura to taste. Add a few decorative ice cubes to the glass, if liked. Finish with tonic water and garnish with frozen lime slices.

Variation
Use fresh lime or grapefruit juice and a splash of sugar syrup instead of the lime cordial, and finish with ginger ale.

Blushing Piña Colada

This is good with or without the rum that is part of the original recipe. Don't be tempted to put whole ice cubes into the blender; the result won't be as smooth and you may ruin the blades. Make sure you crush it well first. The recipe serves two.

1 banana, peeled and sliced
1 thick slice pineapple, peeled
3 measures/4½ tbsp pineapple juice
1 scoop strawberry ice cream or sorbet
1 measure/1½ tbsp unsweetened coconut milk
30ml/2 tbsp grenadine

Roughly chop the banana. Cut two small wedges from the pineapple and set aside. Cut up the remainder of the pineapple and add it to the blender with the banana. Add the pineapple juice and process until smooth.

Add the ice cream or sorbet with the coconut milk and a little finely crushed ice, and process until smooth. Pour into two large cocktail glasses. Pour the grenadine syrup slowly on top of the drink; it will filter down, creating a dappled effect. Garnish each glass with a wedge of pineapple and a cherry.

Steel Works

This thirst-quenching drink can be served at any time of the day.

2 measures/3 tbsp passion fruit juice
dash Angostura bitters
3 measures/4½ tbsp soda water, chilled
3 measures/4½ tbsp lemonade, chilled
1 passion fruit

Pour the passion fruit juice into a tumbler. Add the Angostura, with some ice cubes. Finish the drink with the chilled soda water and lemonade and stir briefly. Cut the passion fruit in half; scoop out the seeds and flesh and add to the drink. Stir gently before serving.

Variation
For a Rock Shandy, pour equal parts of lemonade and soda over bitters or use your favourite variety of the naturally flavoured and unsweetened fruit drinks.

Bandrek

This is a rich and creamy version of a spicy Indonesian drink. Serve it either warm or chilled. If you like, add a very fresh egg to the syrup and mix in the blender, and you'll have something like an egg-nog.

3 whole cloves
3 juniper berries, bruised
1 cinnamon stick
6 green cardamom pods, bruised
4 whole black peppercorns
1 sugar cube
2 measures/3 tbsp unsweetened coconut milk
3 measures/4½ tbsp full-cream (whole) milk

Put the cloves, juniper berries, cinnamon, cardamom pods, peppercorns and sugar cube in a pan. Heat gently to release the aromas and flavours of the spices. Add 175ml/6fl oz water and bring to the boil over medium-high heat. Continue to boil for about ten minutes, or until reduced to 30–45ml/2–3 tbsp of spicy syrup. Remove from the heat and cool. Pour the syrup into a blender with the coconut milk and full-cream milk and process until smooth. Strain over cracked ice in a stemmed glass. Garnish with cinnamon sticks and a maraschino cherry.

St Clements

Oranges and lemons create a simple but thirst-quenching drink, which confirms that freshly squeezed fruit has a superior flavour to any of the ready-squeezed versions you can buy.

2 oranges
1 lemon
15ml/1 tbsp sugar, or to taste
75ml/5 tbsp water

Wash the oranges and lemons and then pare the rind off the fruit with a sharp knife, leaving the white pith behind. Remove the pith from the fruit and discard it. Put the orange and lemon rind in a pan with the sugar and water. Place over low heat and stir gently until the sugar has dissolved. Remove the pan from the heat and press the orange and lemon rind against the sides of the pan to release

all their oils. Cover the pan and let cool. Remove and discard the rind. Purée the oranges and lemon and sweeten the fruit pulp by pouring the cooled citrus syrup over it. Set aside for 2–3 hours to allow the flavours to infuse. Strain the fruit pulp, pressing the solids in the sieve to extract as much of the juice as possible. Pour into a tall glass filled with finely crushed ice, and decorate with slices of orange and lemon.

Fennel Fusion

This hefty combination of raw vegetables and apples makes a surprisingly delicious juice. Cabbage has natural anti-bacterial properties, while apples and fennel can help to cleanse the system.

half a small red cabbage
half a fennel bulb
2 apples
⅔ measure/1 tbsp lemon juice

Roughly slice the cabbage and fennel and quarter the apples. Using a juice extractor, juice the vegetables and fruit. Add the lemon juice to the juice mixture and stir. Pour into a glass and serve.

Summer Tonic

The many nutrients in lettuce include betacarotene, iron and folic acid. This is a particularly appetizing way of getting your share of them.

3 large vine-ripened tomatoes
half a Little Gem (Bibb) lettuce
5cm/2in piece cucumber
1 small garlic clove
small handful fresh parsley, stalks
    included
⅔ measure/1 tbsp lemon juice

Halve the tomatoes and lettuce. Peel and chop the cucumber. Juice all the ingredients together and serve in a tall glass.

Raspberry and Orange Smoothie

This exquisite blend combines the sharp taste of raspberries and oranges with the creaminess of yogurt. It takes minutes to prepare, making it perfect for breakfast. Serves two to three.

250g/9oz raspberries, chilled
200ml/7fl oz natural (plain) yogurt, chilled
300ml/½ pint orange juice, chilled

Place the raspberries and yogurt in a food processor or blender, and process for about a minute until smooth and creamy. Add the orange juice to the raspberry and yogurt mixture and process for about 30 seconds, or until thoroughly combined. Pour into tall glasses and serve immediately.

Avocado and Lime Smoothie

Inspired by guacamole, this wonderfully thick smoothie combines mild and spicy flavours perfectly. It serves four.

3 ripe avocados
juice of 1½ limes
1 garlic clove, crushed
handful of ice cubes
400ml/14fl oz vegetable stock, chilled
400ml/14fl oz full-cream (whole) milk, chilled
150ml/¼ pint sour cream, chilled
few drops Tabasco
salt and ground black pepper
extra virgin olive oil, to serve

For the salsa:
4 tomatoes, peeled, seeded and finely diced
2 spring onions (scallions), finely chopped
1 green chilli, seeded and finely chopped
15ml/1 tbsp chopped fresh coriander (cilantro)

juice of half a lime
salt and ground black pepper

Prepare the salsa first. Mix all the ingredients and season to taste with salt and pepper. Chill while you prepare the smoothie. Halve and stone the avocados. Scoop out the flesh and place in a blender. Add the lime juice, garlic, a handful of crushed ice and about 150ml/¼ pint of the vegetable stock, and process until smooth. Pour the mixture into a large pitcher, and stir in the remaining stock, milk, sour cream, Tabasco and seasoning. Pour the smoothie into glasses and spoon a little salsa on to each. Add a splash of olive oil to each portion and garnish with fresh coriander leaves. Serve immediately, with a spoon.

Georgia 'n' Ginger

This is named after the US state of Georgia, which is famous for its peaches. The recipe serves six.

1 can (450–500g/1–1¼lb) sliced peaches in syrup
750ml/1¼ pints strong coffee
120ml/4fl oz whipping cream
25ml/1½ tbsp brown sugar
1.5ml/¼ tsp ground cinnamon
generous pinch ground ginger

Drain the peaches, retaining the syrup. In a blender, process half of the coffee and the peaches for 1 minute. In a clean bowl, whip the cream. Put 250ml/8fl oz cold water, the sugar, cinnamon, ginger and peach syrup in a pan and bring to the boil over a medium heat, then reduce the heat and simmer for 1 minute. Add the blended peaches and the remaining coffee to the pan and stir well. Serve, topped with whipped cream and decorated with orange rind.

Strawberry Soother

Relax with this comforting strawberry blend, which is rich in vitamin C and healing phytochemicals.

225g/8oz strawberries
1 peach or nectarine

Hull the strawberries, then quarter the peach or nectarine and pull out the stone. Cut the flesh into rough slices or chunks. Juice the fruit, using a juicer, or process in a food processor or blender for a thicker juice, and serve immediately.

Citrus Shake

This refreshing juice is great for boosting the immune system. Citrus fruits are a rich source of vitamin C.

1 pink grapefruit
1 blood orange
30ml/2 tbsp lemon juice

Peel the grapefruit and orange and cut them into rough segments. Juice the fruit, then stir in the lemon juice.

Lemonade on Ice

Home-made lemonade may not be fizzy, but it has a fresh, tangy flavour, unmatched by bought drinks. The basic lemonade will keep well in the refrigerator for up to 2 weeks and makes a thirst-quenching drink at any time of day. This recipe serves six.

6 lemons
225g/8oz caster (superfine) sugar
1.75 litres/3 pints boiling water

For each iced drink:
4 scoops lemon sorbet
thin lemon and lime slices
3 ice cubes, crushed

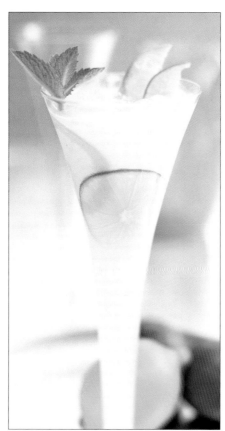

Tropical Soother

This reviving juice helps keep the liver and kidneys good and healthy. Melon is an especially good kidney tonic.

1 papaya
half a cantaloupe melon
90g/3½oz white grapes

Start by making the lemonade. Wash the lemons and dry them thoroughly. Pare all the lemons thinly, avoiding the bitter white pith, and put the rind in a large heatproof bowl. Add the sugar. Squeeze the lemons and set the juice aside. Pour the measured boiling water over the lemon rinds and sugar. Stir until the sugar dissolves. Leave to cool, then stir in the lemon juice. Strain the lemonade into a large jug and chill.

For each glass of iced lemonade, place four scoops of sorbet in a tall glass and tuck some lemon and lime slices down the sides. Add the crushed ice. Top up each glass with about 200ml/7fl oz of the lemonade. Garnish with mint sprigs and half-slices of lemon and lime.

Halve and skin the papaya, then remove the seeds with a spoon and cut into rough slices. Cut open the melon and remove the seeds with a spoon. Cut into quarters and slice the flesh away from the skin, then cut into rough chunks. Juice all the fruit.

Melon Pick-Me-Up

This spicy blend of melon, pear and fresh root ginger will revive your body, stimulate your circulation and fire you into action.

half a cantaloupe melon
2 pears
2.5cm/1in piece fresh root ginger

Quarter the melon, remove the seeds and slice the flesh away from the skin, then quarter the pears. Using a juice extractor, juice all the ingredients, pour into a tall glass and serve immediately.

Apple Shiner

Enjoy radiant skin and instant energy with this cleansing fusion of fresh fruits and lemon juice.

1 apple
half a honeydew melon
90g/3½oz red grapes
⅔ measure/1 tbsp lemon juice

Quarter the apple and remove the core. Cut the melon into quarters, remove the seeds and slice the flesh away from the skin. Using a juice extractor, juice the fruit. Alternatively, process the fruit in a food processor or blender for 2–3 minutes until smooth. Pour the juice into a chilled glass, stir in the lemon juice and serve.

Green Leaves

This healthy juice is exceptionally rejuvenating. Grapes are one of the most effective detoxifiers, and are used for alleviating many kinds of skin, liver and kidney disorders.

1 apple
150g/5oz white grapes

small handful fresh coriander (cilantro)
30g/1oz watercress
⅔ measure/1 tbsp lime juice

Quarter the apple. Juice the fruit, coriander and watercress, then stir in the lime juice. If you find this mixture too sour, use less lime.

Humzinger

This tropical cleanser will help boost the digestive system and the kidneys, making your eyes sparkle, your hair shine and your skin glow.

half a pineapple, peeled
1 small mango, peeled and pitted
half a small papaya, seeded and peeled

Use a sharp knife to remove any "eyes" left in the pineapple, and cut all the fruit into rough chunks. Using a juice extractor, juice the fruit. Alternatively, use a food processor or blender and process for 2–3 minutes until very smooth. Pour into a glass and serve immediately.

Cranberry, Cinnamon and Ginger Spritzer

Partially freezing fruit juice gives it a wonderfully slushy texture that is very refreshing. The combination of cranberry and apple juice contributes a tart, clean flavour that's not too sweet. Serves four.

600ml/1 pint chilled cranberry juice
150ml/¼ pint clear apple juice
4 cinnamon sticks
about 400ml/14fl oz chilled ginger ale

Pour the cranberry juice into a shallow freezerproof container and freeze for about two hours, or until a thick layer of ice crystals has formed around the edges. Mash with a fork to break up the ice, then return the mixture to the freezer for a further 2–3 hours until almost solid. Pour the apple juice into a small pan, add two cinnamon sticks and bring to just below boiling point. Pour into a pitcher and leave to cool, then remove the cinnamon sticks and set them aside with the other cinnamon sticks. Chill the juice until very cold. Spoon the cranberry ice into a food processor. Add the apple juice and blend very briefly until slushy. Pile into cocktail glasses or flutes, top up with chilled ginger ale and garnish with fresh or frozen cranberries. Put a long cinnamon stick into each glass to use as a swizzle-stick.

Super Clean

This delicious drink will really kick-start your system. Carrots are a key detox vegetable: they cleanse, nourish and stimulate the body.

3 carrots
30g/1oz young spinach
115g/4oz cooked beetroot in natural juice
2 celery sticks

Top and tail the carrots. Process all the ingredients in a blender until smooth, then pour into a glass and serve.

Bartending know-how
Beetroot is another key vegetable in cleansing the system. Like carrot, it is exceptionally good for the liver. Always use fresh beetroot (not the sliced pickled stuff that comes in jars). Not only does it add rich, lustrous colour to a vegetable juice blend, but it also contributes a pronounced degree of natural sweetness to the drink.

Iced Mango Lassi

Based on a traditional Indian drink, this is excellent with spicy food, or as a welcome cooler at any time of day. The recipe serves three to four.

For the yogurt ice:
175g/6oz caster (superfine) sugar
150ml/¼ pint water
2 lemons
500ml/17fl oz Greek yogurt

For each drink:
4 measures/6 tbsp mango juice

To make the yogurt ice, put the sugar and water in a pan and heat gently, stirring occasionally, until the sugar has dissolved. Pour the syrup into a pitcher. Leave to cool, then chill until very cold. Grate the lemons and squeeze them. Add the rind and juice to the chilled syrup and stir well to mix.

By hand: Pour the syrup mixture into a container and freeze until thickened. Beat in the yogurt, and return to the freezer until thick enough to scoop.

If using an ice cream maker: Churn the mixture until it thickens. Stir in the yogurt and churn for 2 minutes more until well mixed. Transfer to a plastic tub or similar freezerproof container and freeze.

To make each lassi, briefly blend the mango juice with three small scoops of the yogurt ice in a food processor or blender until just smooth. Pour the mixture into a tall glass or tumbler and add a few ice cubes. Top each drink with another scoop of the yogurt ice and garnish with fresh mint sprigs and mango wedges. Serve at once.

Tropical Fruit Soda

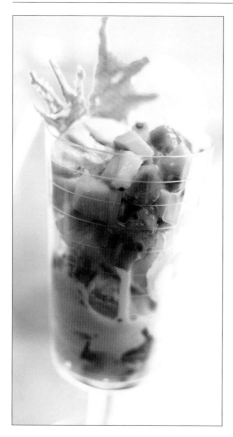

For many children, scoops of vanilla ice cream served in a froth of lemonade would make the perfect treat. This more elaborate version, with its tropical fruit content, will appeal to adults too. It serves four.

10ml/2 tsp sugar
1 papaya
1 small ripe mango
2 passion fruit
8 large scoops vanilla ice cream
8 large scoops caramel or toffee ice cream
about 400ml/14fl oz chilled lemonade or
   soda water

Line a baking sheet with foil. Make four small mounds of sugar on the foil, using about 2.5ml/½ tsp each time and spacing them well apart. Place under a medium grill (broiler) for about two minutes until the sugar mounds have turned to a pale golden caramel. Immediately swirl each pool of caramel with the tip of a cocktail stick or skewer to give a slightly feathery finish. Leave to cool.

Cut the papaya in half. Scoop out and discard the seeds, then remove the skin and chop the flesh. Skin the mango, cut the flesh off the stone and chop it into bitesize chunks. Mix the papaya and mango in a bowl. Cut each passion fruit in half, and scoop the pulp into the bowl of fruit. Mix well, cover and chill until ready to serve.

Divide the chilled fruit mixture among four large tumblers. Add one scoop of each type of ice cream to each glass. Peel the caramel decorations carefully away from the foil and press gently into the ice cream. Top up with lemonade or soda water and serve.

Yellow Pepper Revitalizer

This vibrant fresh fruit and vegetable combination will help to rejuvenate and revitalize your body. It is rich in immune-boosting vitamin C, protective betacarotene and energizing natural fruit sugars. As well as these handy attributes, it also tastes sensational – zesty, crisp, fresh and naturally sweet.

3 carrots
1 apple
1 yellow pepper

Scrub and trim the carrots and quarter the apple. Roughly chop the pepper. Using a juice extractor, juice all the ingredients, pour into a glass and serve immediately.

Revitalizer

This classic combination will benefit those suffering from constipation and arthritis. Natural fruit sugars will provide a boost of energy.

3 carrots
1 apple
1 orange

Top and tail the carrots, then quarter the apple. Peel the orange and cut into rough segments. Juice the carrots and fruit.

Licuado de Melon

Among the most refreshing drinks Mexicans make are fruit extracts mixed with honey and chilled water. This recipe is enough for four.

1 watermelon
1 litre/1¾ pints chilled water
juice of 2 limes
honey

Cut the watermelon flesh into chunks, discarding the black seeds. Cover with chilled water and leave for 10 minutes. Tip the mixture into a large sieve set over a bowl. Using a wooden spoon, press the fruit to extract all the liquid. Stir in the lime juice and sweeten with honey. Pour into a pitcher, add ice cubes and stir. Serve in tumblers.

Strawberry Kiss

A new spin on strawberries and cream, this makes a superb opener to a summer lunch.

12 strawberries
1½ measure/2 tsp lemon juice
½ measure/2 tsp whipping cream
2.5ml/½ tsp caster (superfine) sugar

Liquidize all the ingredients with a handful of crushed ice, and turn out into a wine glass. Garnish with a whole small strawberry.

Citrus Agua Fresca

These refreshing fruit juices are sold from street stalls in towns all over Mexico. The recipe serves four.

12 limes
3 oranges
2 grapefruit
600ml/1 pint water
75g/6 tbsp caster (superfine) sugar

Squeeze the juice from the fruits. Some fruit pulp should be used, but discard the seeds. Pour the mixture into a large pitcher. Add the water and sugar and stir until all the sugar has dissolved. Chill for at least an hour before serving with ice and extra fruit wedges. The drink will keep for up to a week in a covered container in the refrigerator.

Tamarind Agua Fresca

Sometimes referred to as the Indian date, tamarind is native to Asia and North Africa, and has now travelled to Mexico. It is used medicinally and as an antiseptic. The fruit has a sweet-sour taste and makes a drink similar to lemonade. This recipe serves four.

1 litre/1¾ pints water
225g/8oz tamarind pods
25g/2 tbsp caster (superfine) sugar

Pour the water into a pan and heat until warm. Remove from the heat and pour into a bowl. Peel the tamarind pods and add the pulp to the warm water. Soak for at least four hours. Place a sieve over a clean bowl. Pour the tamarind pulp and water into the sieve, then press the pulp through the sieve with the back of a wooden spoon, leaving the black seeds behind. Discard the seeds. Add the sugar to the tamarind mixture and stir well until dissolved. Pour into a pitcher and chill thoroughly before serving in tumblers filled with ice.

Bartending know-how
Jars of tamarind pulp or paste are available for buying at Indian and Asian food stores.

Pineapple and Lime Agua Fresca

The vivid colours of this fresh fruit drink give some indication of its wonderful flavour. It makes a delicious midday refresher or pick-me-up at the end of a hard day. The recipe serves four.

2 pineapples
juice of 2 limes
475ml/16fl oz still mineral water
50g/2oz caster (superfine) sugar

Peel the pineapples and chop the flesh, removing the core and "eyes" (see below). You should have about 450g/1lb flesh. Put this in a food processor or blender, and add the lime juice and half the mineral water. Purée to a smooth pulp. Stop the machine and scrape the mixture from the side of the goblet once or twice during processing. Place a sieve over a large bowl. Tip the pineapple pulp into the sieve and press it through with a wooden spoon. Pour the sieved mixture into a large pitcher, cover and chill in the refrigerator for about an hour. Stir in the remaining mineral water and sugar to taste. Serve with ice.

Bartending know-how
Remove pineapple skin with a deep spiral action to cut out the "eyes".

Granita di Caffè

This is basically coffee ice, or slush.
The recipe serves four.

200ml/7fl oz strong coffee (about five
    generous cups of espresso or filter/
    cafetière brewed coffee using 80g/14 tbsp
    coffee per 1 litre/1¾ pints water)
400ml/14fl oz water
140g/5oz sugar
2.5ml/½ tsp vanilla essence (extract)
1 egg white (optional)
120ml/4fl oz whipped cream

Pour the brewed coffee into a large
bowl and set aside. Boil half the water
with the sugar, stirring to dissolve.
Refrigerate. When the sugar syrup is
cold, add it, the remaining water, and
the vanilla to the coffee. Stir until well
blended. If using, whisk the egg white
and fold it into the mixture. Pour the
mixture into a shallow freezerproof tin,
such as an ice-cube tray or baking
sheet, and freeze. About every 30
minutes, break the mixture up with a
fork to create the traditional, grainy,
shaved-ice consistency. When it is well
frozen, serve in individual cups, and
top them with a little whipped cream.

Mexican Coffee

The Aztec Indians were the first known
chocolate aficionados, and chocolate is
an ingredient in many Mexican recipes.
Combined with coffee, it makes a rich,
smooth drink. This recipe does four.

30ml/2 tbsp chocolate syrup
120ml/4fl oz whipping cream
1.5ml/¼ tsp ground cinnamon
25g/2 tbsp brown sugar
pinch ground nutmeg
475ml/16fl oz strong black coffee
whipped cream

Whip together the chocolate syrup,
cream, cinnamon, sugar and nutmeg.
Pour the hot coffee into the mixture and
stir, before dividing among four mugs.
Top with a dollop of whipped cream
and garnish with shavings of cinnamon.

Coffee-Chocolate Soda

This is a fun, refreshing drink that tastes
as good as it looks. The combination
of chocolate ice cream and coffee-
flavoured fizz makes for an unusually
textured but thoroughly exciting
cocktail. The recipe serves two.

250ml/8fl oz strong cold coffee
60ml/4 tbsp double (heavy) cream, or 30ml/
    2 tbsp evaporated (unsweetened
    condensed) milk (optional)
250ml/8fl oz cold soda water
2 scoops chocolate ice cream
chocolate-covered coffee beans, roughly
    chopped, to garnish

Pour the coffee into tall glasses. Add
the cream or evaporated milk, if using.
Add the soda water and stir. Gently
place a scoop of ice cream into the
mixture. Garnish with some of the
roughly chopped chocolate-covered
coffee beans. Serve with a long spoon
or a straw.

Variation
Try also chocolate mint, vanilla,
hazelnut or banana ice cream and
sprinkle with chocolate shavings,
fruit slices or even a few roughly
chopped pieces of hazelnut.

Chilled Coffee Caribbean

Use coffee that is not too strong. Filter
coffee gives a clean, clear texture.
Serves two.

600ml/1 pint strong filter coffee, cooled for
    about 20 minutes
half an orange and half an lemon, thinly sliced
1 pineapple slice
sugar, to taste
1–2 drops Angostura bitters (optional)

Add the cooled coffee to the fruit slices
in a large bowl. Stir and chill in the
freezer for about an hour or until very
cold. Remove from the freezer and stir
again. Remove the fruit slices from the
liquid. Add sugar to taste, and stir in
the bitters, if using. Add three ice cubes
per drink to tall glasses, or whisky
tumblers, then pour over the chilled
coffee drink. Garnish with half-slices of
orange or lemon.

Cappuccino

There can be nothing more enjoyable than a steaming hot cup of coffee on a cold winter's day. This is the classic espresso and milk drink, to serve two.

160–250ml/5½–8fl oz very cold full-cream (whole) milk
about 15g/½oz dark-roast espresso coffee, finely ground

Pour very cold milk into a metal pitcher or frothing device, steam until a fine, smooth foam has formed, and set aside. Next, brew two cups of espresso, and pour into cappuccino or regular coffee cups. Pour the steamed milk over the coffee, holding back the froth with a spoon until last, when it can be spooned on to the surface.

The ideal cappuccino should be about one-third each espresso coffee, steamed milk and frothed milk. (After brewing the coffee you may need to re-steam the milk for just a moment if it has begun to "fall", or lose the froth.) Top with a sprinkle of chocolate or cocoa powder, if desired.

Caffè Latte

This is a very basic breakfast drink, as served in homes and bars throughout Italy and France. It can be made with only a manual espresso pot and a pan to heat the milk. Serves two.

2 parts espresso or very strong coffee
6 parts boiled milk
sugar (optional)
steamed, frothed milk for topping (optional)

Pour the brewed coffee into glasses or large French coffee bowls. Add the hot milk and sugar, if using, and stir well. Top each glass with a spoonful of steamed, frothed milk if desired.

Bartending know-how
If you are having a period of abstinence from caffeine, be assured that the decaffeinated versions of coffee are much improved these days. Carbonated water is now the only decaffeinating agent.

Café di Olla

This recipe is traditionally brewed in large quantities over a wood fire in a heavy earthenware Mexican cooking pot, called an *olla*. It serves four.

1 litre/1¾ pints water
150g/5oz dark brown sugar
5ml/1 tsp molasses
1 small cinnamon stick
50g/2oz dark-roast coffee, medium grind
aniseeds (optional)

Place the water, sugar, molasses, cinnamon and aniseeds, if using, in a pan and slowly bring to the boil. Stir thoroughly to dissolve the sugar and molasses. When the mixture reaches boiling point, stir in the dry coffee, remove from the heat, cover, and steep for 5 minutes. Strain into earthenware mugs and serve immediately. Add a few of the aniseeds, for that extra touch of spice.

Normandy Coffee

Like Washington State in the USA and England's West Country, Normandy is known for its apple orchards, and gives it name to many dishes made with apple juice or apple sauce. This recipe blends the flavour of apples with spices for a delicious, tangy coffee drink. It serves four.

475ml/16fl oz strong black coffee (espresso strength, or filter/cafetière brewed at 75g/ 13 tbsp coffee per 1 litre/1¾ pints water)
475ml/16fl oz apple juice
25g/2 tbsp brown sugar, to taste
3 oranges, thinly sliced
2 small cinnamon sticks
pinch ground allspice
pinch ground cloves

Bring all the ingredients to the boil over a medium heat, then reduce the heat and simmer for 10 minutes. Strain the liquid into a preheated flask or serving pitcher. Pour into cappuccino-style cups, adding a cinnamon stick to each, if you wish.

Bartending know-how
Use a French or Viennese roast coffee – dark but not as dark as for espresso, so that the spice and molasses aren't overwhelmed.

Café con Leche

Many Mexicans start the day with this spiced milky coffee, and those who have enjoyed a hearty midday meal will often opt for a cup of it with a pastry as the afternoon snack. This recipe serves four.

50g/2oz ground coffee
475ml/16fl oz boiling water
475ml/16fl oz full-cream (whole) milk
4 cinnamon sticks
sugar, to taste

Make up the coffee in a cafetière. Pour the milk into a heavy pan, add the cinnamon sticks and bring to the boil, stirring occasionally. Using a slotted spoon, lift out the cinnamon sticks and use a smaller spoon to press down on them to release any liquid they have absorbed. Set the cinnamon sticks aside for serving. Add the coffee to the hot milk, then pour into cups. Add a cinnamon stick to each cup. Drinkers should add sugar to taste.

Horchata

This delicious, aromatic rice drink tastes wonderfully creamy, yet does not contain a drop of milk. Mexicans swear by it as a means of settling stomach upsets or curing hangovers, and it is often served at breakfast. This recipe makes four.

450g/1lb long grain rice
750ml/1¼ pints water
150g/5oz blanched whole almonds
10ml/2 tsp ground cinnamon
finely grated rind of a lime
50g/2oz caster (superfine) sugar

Tip the rice into a sieve and rinse thoroughly under cold running water. Drain, tip into a large bowl and pour over the water. Cover and soak for at least two hours and preferably overnight. Drain the rice, reserving 600ml/1 pint of the soaking liquid. Spoon the rice into a food processor or blender and grind as finely as possible. Add the almonds to the processor or blender and continue to grind in the same way until finely ground. Add the cinnamon, grated lime rind and sugar to the ground rice and ground almonds. Add the reserved soaking water from the rice and mix until all the sugar has dissolved. Serve in tall glasses with ice cubes. Garnish with strips of lime rind.

Coffee Milkshake

This cold coffee drink does not require a blender. The recipe serves two.

200ml/7fl oz chilled strong coffee (four cups espresso, or filter/cafetière brewed using 70g/ 12 tbsps coffee per 1 litre/1¾ pints water)
2 eggs, well-beaten
450ml/¾ pint cold milk
100ml/3½fl oz single (light) or double (heavy) cream
15ml/1 tbsp sugar
pinch of salt
4 drops vanilla or almond essence (extract)

Mix the ingredients in a shaker. Serve at once, sprinkled with ginger cookies.

Atole

This drink, which is made from tehe white corn, *masa harina*, is traditionally flavoured with *piloncillo* (Mexican unrefined brown sugar) and ground cinnamon. It has the consistency of a thick milkshake. Fresh fruit purées are often added before serving and some recipes introduce ground almonds or milk. This one serves six.

200g/7oz white *masa harina*
1.2 litres/2 pints water
1 vanilla pod
50g/2oz *piloncillo*, or soft dark brown sugar
2.5ml/½ tsp ground cinnamon
115g/4oz fresh strawberries, chopped pineapple or orange segments (optional)

Put the *masa harina* in a heavy pan and gradually beat in the water to make a smooth paste. Place the pan over a medium heat, add the vanilla pod and bring the mixture to the boil, stirring constantly until it thickens. Beat in the sugar and ground cinnamon and continue to beat until the sugar has dissolved. Remove from the heat. If adding the fruit, purée it in a food processor or blender until smooth, and then press the purée through a sieve. Stir the purée into the corn mixture and return to the heat until warmed through. Remove the vanilla pod. Serve.

Champurrada

This popular version of Atole is made with Mexican chocolate. A special wooden whisk called a *molinollo* is traditionally used when making this frothy drink. The recipe serves six.

115g/4oz Mexican chocolate
1.2 litres/2 pints water or milk, or a mixture
200g/7oz white *masa harina*
25g/2 tbsp soft dark brown sugar

Put the chocolate in a mortar and grind with a pestle until it becomes a fine powder. Alternatively, grind the chocolate in a food processor. Put the liquid in a heavy pan and gradually stir in all the *masa harina* until a smooth paste is formed. Use a traditional wooden *molinollo* or a wire whisk for a frothier drink. Place the pan over a medium heat and bring the mixture to the boil, stirring all the time until the frothy drink thickens. Stir in the ground chocolate, then add the sugar. Serve immediately.

Mexican Hot Chocolate

This sumptuous version of hot chocolate relies on the beguiling flavours of almond, cloves and cinnamon for its sweetly spicy appeal. The recipe serves four.

1 litre/1¾ pints full-cream (whole) milk
1 cinnamon stick
2 whole cloves
115g/4oz plain dark chocolate, chopped into small pieces
2–3 drops almond essence (extract)

Heat the milk gently with the spices in a pan until almost boiling, then stir in the chocolate over a medium heat until melted. Strain into a blender, add the almond essence and whizz on high speed for about 30 seconds until frothy. Pour into warmed heatproof glasses and serve immediately.

Iced Mint and Chocolate Cooler

This makes a stimulating alternative to dessert, and is in a different class altogether to mint-choc-chip ice cream. The recipe serves four.

60ml/4 tbsp drinking chocolate
400ml/14fl oz full-cream (whole) milk
150ml/¼ pint natural (plain) yogurt
2.5ml/½ tsp peppermint essence (extract)
4 scoops chocolate ice cream

Place the drinking chocolate in a small pan and stir in about 120ml/4fl oz of the milk. Heat gently, stirring, until almost boiling, then remove the pan from the heat. Pour the hot chocolate milk into a heatproof bowl or large pitcher and whisk in the remaining milk, Add the yogurt and peppermint essence and whisk again. Pour the mixture into four tall glasses, filling them no more than three-quarters full. Top each drink with a scoop of ice cream. Garnish with mint leaves and chocolate shapes. Serve immediately.

Coffee Frappé

Similar to a milkshake, this frappé recipe is another long, cold coffee drink that is both refreshing and uplifting. The recipe serves two.

450ml/¾ pint cold strong coffee (brewed using about 80g/14 tbsp coffee per 1 litre/1¾ pints water)
8 drops vanilla essence (extract)
60ml/4 tbsp condensed milk
sugar, to taste

Add the cold brewed coffee to a large blender. Next, add the vanilla essence, a couple of handfuls of crushed ice and the condensed milk. Blend well until a smooth texture is obtained. Pour into tall, clear glasses, and stir in sugar to taste. Garnish with some whipped cream and banana slices, if you wish.

GLOSSARY

What follows is a list of the generic terms most frequently encountered in the cocktail world.

ABV: Stands for "alcohol by volume", and shows the total percentage within the drink that is accounted for by pure ethyl alcohol. All alcoholic products must, by law, give this information.

Aperitif: Any drink taken before eating as a stimulant to the appetite. Can be as simple as a glass of dry white wine, champagne or sherry. Can also be a dry or sour cocktail.

Cobbler: A long drink consisting of spirit with sugar and ice, served with plenty of fruit to garnish. American in origin, it is the forerunner of all lavishly garnished cocktails.

Chaser: A longer drink that is taken immediately after a small one, typically a glass of beer to follow a shot of neat spirit. It soothes the throat after the high alcohol of its predecessor.

*Below: Champagne is an excellent **aperitif** for whetting the appetite.*

*Above: A **cup** makes a refreshing, long drink as a party starter. They are generally lavishly garnished with fruit.*

Collins: A long drink originally called the Tom Collins after a particular variety of gin. A Collins is now any spirit mixed with lemon juice and sugar, and topped up with soda. It is basically a long version of the Sour.

Cooler: An indeterminate long drink that consists of any spirit with fruit juice (usually citrus), sugar and a sparkling topper (which may be soda, lemonade or ginger ale). Classically decorated with a spiral citrus twist.

Crusta: Any drink that comes in a glass with a frosted rim, usually of sugar (although the salt-rimmed Margarita is theoretically a Crusta too). Should also technically be served with a continuous twist of lemon rind lining the glass.

Cup: Essentially the cold version of Punch, a Cup is a mixture of wine or cider with spirits and fruit juices, served from a large bowl full of fruit garnishes and ice. Best served in summer.

Daisy: A soured spirit that also contains a measure of fruit syrup such as grenadine, topped up with soda.

Egg-nog: A long mixture of spirit or fortified wine with whole egg, sugar and milk, served cold and usually seasoned with nutmeg. Traditional as a Christmas drink in the USA.

Fix: Virtually the same thing as a Daisy. Consists of spirit, lemon juice, a fruit syrup and a sparkling topper, but with the Fix, it is essential to put the squeezed lemon rind into the drink.

Fizz: Almost any long drink topped up with soda, but classically just spirit, lemon juice, sugar and soda, perhaps with a drop of egg white to help the texture. Buck's Fizz, a champagne drink, marked a radical departure for the Fizz.

Flip: A short drink containing egg, sugar and either spirit or fortified wine, usually seasoned with nutmeg. Similar to an egg-nog, but without the milk.

Frappé: Any drink that is served over a snow of finely crushed ice.

*Below: A gin and lemon **fizz** topped with fruit and flower ice cubes.*

*Above: A tall glass can be used for fruity drinks served **on the rocks**.*

Highball: Simply spirit with ice, topped up with soda or some other sparkling mixer, but with no other ingredient.

Julep: A hot-weather American drink, served in a tall glass. Consists of spirit (classically bourbon) and plenty of crushed ice, on a base of mint leaves pressed with sugar. As the ice melts, it becomes a long drink.

Mulling: The technique of gently heating wine, beer or cider with spices, fruit and perhaps a shot of spirit. To be served hot during the British Christmas season.

Neat: Any spirit drunk on its own without ice or mixer. "As it comes" is the synonymous phrase.

On the rocks: Any drink served over ice cubes or cracked ice, usually in a tumbler or Old-Fashioned glass.

Pick-me-up: Any drink whose purpose is to revive the drinker, whether in mid-morning or to counteract the effects of over-indulgence. It is a bit of a loaded term, since it shouldn't be forgotten that all alcohol depresses the central nervous system, rather than "picks it up".

Pousse-café: A small cocktail in which two or more ingredients are poured slowly into the glass one by one to create a layered effect. Must be served without ice or garnishes.

Punch: An old British colonial drink consisting of spirits and wine, heated up with spices and fruit, and served from a large bowl. Similar to mulled wine, and likewise traditionally served at Christmas.

Rickey: A unsweetened measure of spirit with lime juice and ice, topped up with soda.

Sangaree: May be based on a spirit, but is usually fortified wine with sugar, soda and a nutmeg topping.

Shooter: A small, strong cocktail served in a shot glass, intended to be downed in one. Historically, any tot of neat spirit taken in the same way.

*Below: A **pousse-café** layered with Kahlúa, Bailey's Irish Cream and Grand Marnier.*

*Above: A **sour** made from gin, fresh lemon juice and a pinch of sugar.*

Shrub: A drink consisting of spirit (usually brandy or rum) bottled with fruit juices and loaf (or lump) sugar, and left to infuse for several weeks.

Sling: A long drink consisting of spirit with lemon juice, sugar and soda. Similar to a Collins, it now generally contains a shot of some liqueur as well.

Smash: An undersized version of the Julep, made with ground mint, sugar and spirit, but served in a small glass and with not as much ice.

Sour: Any spirit mixed with lemon juice and a pinch of sugar, sometimes taken with a small splash of soda, but always as a short drink.

Swizzle: Cocktail of Caribbean origin involving spirit, lime juice, bitters, sugar and ice, frothed up by being vigorously stirred with a swizzle-stick held between the palms of the hands. Must be served Antarctically cold.

Toddy: A cold-weather drink consisting of spirit, lemon juice and sugar (or perhaps honey), to which hot water is added. Implicitly believed in as a cold remedy by previous generations.

INDEX

Figures in **bold** refer to main references

Acknowledgements

The publisher would like
to thank Danes Ltd
(tel. 01273 674 022;
www.danesltd.co.uk)
for supplying Kikor, Poncino
Livornese and Monasterium
bottles for photography.

The publisher would also like to
thank the following for the use of
their pictures in the book (l=left,
r=right, t=top, b=bottom).
AKG: 6, 7t and b, 8t and b;
Cephas: 9b; **Tim Ellerby**: 9t.